How it Was

Leslie Adams

authorHOUSE®

AuthorHouse™ UK Ltd.
500 Avebury Boulevard
Central Milton Keynes, MK9 2BE
www.authorhouse.co.uk
Phone: 08001974150

First published by AuthorHouse 12/9/2009

ISBN: 978-1-4490-4983-6 (sc)

This book is printed on acid-free paper.

In November 1928, and in her early forties when Isabella thought that she was safe from pregnancy at last, she gave birth to her eighth child, another daughter. Having run out of names, the attending midwife happily obliged by calling the child Phyllis. Another mouth to feed and she was now a widow.

Isabella had been married twice. Her first husband was killed in the 1914-18 war leaving her with four children, one of which died at the age of three years. Her second husband died of madness brought on by swallowing unlimited quantities of alcohol, leaving her with another four. Isabella felt no grief or sorrow for her second husband who had been a wife-beater, womaniser, and had left her penniless with no means of support, and no widow's pension because he was eight stamps short on his employment card. (She had always had to carry a Police Whistle in her purse with her everywhere, and when her husband was coming home drunk, one of the neighbours would come to the house to warn her. Isabella would then have to hastily gather the children together and run away for safety until he was sober. He always managed to find her.) When he died she appealed to the Guardians for help and was told to sell any furniture she could, before they would allow her a shilling a week for her and her family to live on.

I was that eighth child, and was soon aware of the great struggle my mother had to feed, clothe, house, and raise her family. She did this in many ways., by taking in laundry and sewing, going out cleaning and tackling any job available. Hers was an extremely hard life but fortunately she was a strong woman both mentally and physically. A woman to be admired and greatly loved. (Mother was never one to waste time gossiping but she was definitely not unsociable. She simply kept herself to herself, was quiet and well-spoken, and was ever ready to help when needed.)

1

My half-brother George was twenty when I was born. When I was two years old I became an Aunt for the first time, and after that during my growing years along came many nieces and nephews. Being the youngest member of the family, and quite timid I always felt rather intimidated and slightly nervous of my half-brothers and sister, especially my half-brothers, having no father and not being used to male domination.

We lived In a small two bed roomed, poorly furnished council house on a large Estate In East London. There was no bathroom or running hot water. The bath was in the kitchen underneath a let-down table top, by the side of the large cast-iron copper with a fire-place beneath to heat the water. (Mother used to use this copper to boil the white linen bed-sheets on washing day as well.) A small toilet was nearby in the passage.

I can remember that we, as did most people in those days, had an old pianoforte, and on a Saturday evening the whole family would gather together and provide their own entertainment. My youngest half-brother Alec on the drums, the older, George playing the piano, while Bella played the Accordion. Everyone joined in with the singing. I would sit listening on the floor by the piano and George would look down and ask me if there was a song he could play for me. I always asked for "Alice Blue Gown", or "My Bonnie", the only two songs that at that time I had learned and liked.

To enable my mother to go out to work I was placed in a local nursery, and can still recall how much I hated it there as if it was only yesterday. When I was five years old however, I went to the Infants School and quite enjoyed it, but I was always a "loner" especially at "playtime". As I was considered to be well-behaved and good at my lessons, I was often allowed to play with a large dolls-house situated along the corridor. I caught Diphtheria from my eldest sister Edith when I was six and was rushed to an Isolation Hospital, remaining there for many weeks. There were of course no visitors allowed, but I remember my mother standing outside and knocking on the window waving to me. In the long children's ward there wasn't any kind of amusement, no books, comics or toys, so as our health slowly improved we used to roll up large sheets of paper or cardboard, tie them with string and throw them across from bed to bed to each other, for something to do.

Many of the children were discharged from the hospital on the same day I was and their parents collected them in big shiny black cars. My mother collected me in an old dilapidated perambulator, and walked all the way home which was a fair distance away, pushing me. I remember feeling terribly embarrassed as I was taken along through streets of shoppers and onlookers, as I was definitely not a baby needing a pram, and at that time did not fully understand the reason for her action. I do now. There was no way she could have afforded a car or taxi to collect me.

I returned to my class at the Infants School and thankfully pleased both my mother and teacher by quickly catching up with the other pupils. As I could read and write quite well at the age of seven I used to walk two or three miles to a free children's library to get books out. I was frequently told by my brother and sisters that I always had my head stuck in a book, and still do when I can. My recollection of Junior School is one of a maze of learning arithmetic and sitting at a desk saying "tables" out loud with the rest of the class over and over again, until they became embedded in my mind. A kind of "Brain Washing" they would call it these days. I hated arithmetic and still do, but loved literature, English, and music. (There were male 'Truant Officers' who cycled the streets of the towns to catch any children who were not attending school.)

My brother, two sisters and I all had household chores to perform to assist our mother. There were many errands to run and I did a great number of them. I recall as a special tea-time treat, going along to the grocers for a pennyworth of broken biscuits, or two pennyworths of stale cakes. The bread we bought was always somewhat cheaper because it was "yesterdays". When cut into slices and spread with dripping it was quite enjoyable and filling. On occasions I would call at the butchers for the bones left over from joints of meat, then to the greengrocers for two pennyworths of Potherbs to make stew. We never had fresh milk because there was no way of keeping it fresh in those days , so we had tins of condensed. Mother often told us about the way George when he was a boy, kept piercing a hole in the bottom of the tins and drinking them until they were empty. He then plugged the holes somehow very neatly, and when they were opened for use they were of course found by her to be empty. She used to take the tins back to the Grocer and complain, until the holes were eventually discovered. (I too loved the sweet taste of it, and if there wasn't anyone around, would spread it onto a slice of bread.)

When in due time we managed to possess a small wireless set and money was available, I then had to carry the Accumulator along to the shop to be charged.   I remember having to be extremely careful with it because of the acid it contained.   I also recall that we had an old wind-up gramophone which we loved to use with a couple of cheap records which we played over and over again.(I shall never forget that my eldest sister Edith, who was currently at work, frequently sent me to the bakers for a three half-penny chocolate cream bun, and then made me sit and watch her eat it.). These things are apt to stay in one's mind. There was of course very little traffic to worry about in those days just buses, bicycles, horses and carts, and a few motor cars. There were trams, but these were used in the

City. One task I really enjoyed doing was Black-leading the fire-range. It shone so beautifully afterwards, especially with a lovely fire going. Then polishing the linoleum which did not fully cover the living room but was edged with large pieces of brown paper or newspaper. Mother used to weave rugs using canvas sacking and old rags, they were lovely and warm to walk on. I can also recall cutting up small pieces of newspaper into squares for use as toilet paper. We helped as much as possible in the house and in the garden. One thing I really hated was when mother gave me a shovel and bucket and sent me out into the middle of the street to collect the dung left by a passing horse and cart, it was so terribly embarrassing and I always felt as if everyone in the neighbouring houses were watching me. I could have died! Mother just knew, and insisted, that it was good manure for the garden. As when the coalman accidentally left any coal in the street from his cart, one of us would have to go out and get it.

There was a Rag and Bone man who used to come around the streets giving baby chicks or gold-fish in exchange for rags or old bottles. Sometimes he had a Roundabout on the back of his cart for the children. Another thing I hated was when one of mother's in-laws from her first marriage would come to visit from London, and take everyone to the local Public House for a drink, leaving me outside looking after a perambulator full of baby nieces and nephews. Luckily it didn't happen very often. I was terrified and quite disgusted even at that young age being near a Public House and drunken men.

My half-brothers George and Alec married and left home, giving my brother Fred the large back bedroom all to himself, while the rest of the family had to share the front one. My mother, sister Elsie and I all slept in the double bed, while Edith, and quite often Bella when she had had a row with her husband, which was a frequent occurrence, shared the single bed. Elsie and I were always sent up to bed early and I remember her singing lots of her school songs to me to settle me down, I loved them and can still recall the words. It wasn't long though before mother would shout out from the foot of the stairs, "You go to bed to sleep", and we would have to be quiet. (I can also remember sitting on the floor at my mother's feet when she had a few minutes to spare, while she sang many of the old Music Hall Songs to me and talked about stars like Vesta Tilley, Marie Lloyd, and George Elliot etc.,. I really loved to hear them and she had such a sweet voice.) There was only three years difference between Elsie and I, and I adored her. We seemed to get on so well together. Edith was very different and hard to like or get on with. For one thing she was always telling false tales about the rest of us to mother and getting us into trouble. I recall the day she told mother that I was upstairs smoking, mother charged up the stairs after me and found that I hadn't even seen a cigarette. As we never received pocket money and hadn't a farthing in our pockets, I don't know how I was supposed to have bought them either, that is if Id wanted them, and I didn't. Mother was very strict with us and of course had to be, but was always very fair. There were a few occasions when she had to resort to physical means of discipline such as the cane on our legs or a clout around the ears, but we no doubt deserved it and it did us no harm whatsoever. In fact it did a lot of good. I recall once when I was very young I was sitting on the mat in front of the fire when mother stood Elsie in front of her and gave her a long quiet lecture about taking money from her purse to buy a pretty tiny basket-weave cot containing a baby doll from a local shop. When she finished talking mother took hold of the toy and threw it into the fire. Elsie burst into tears and I saw the lovely little cot eaten up by the flames, it was so sad, but the message went home. In mother's eyes, manners, politeness, and good behaviour were extremely important. We were also taught to have great respect for our elders and betters, not to speak out of turn, and definitely to give up our seats in buses or trains for adults. Not that we rode in either very often, except when mother managed to treat us to a day out at Southend, which was a special and rare occasion. Although I remember Edith, I really don't know how, talking mother into letting her take me to Clacton for a whole week one summer. I soon discovered that it was for the sole purpose of spending sometime with a boyfriend. On our first day at Clacton Edith took me to the beach, borrowed a large Beach Ball from a nearby holidaymaker and took a photograph of me sitting there holding the ball, for mother to see. From then on she used to leave me in the vicinity of the boarding house every morning playing with the son of the owner, and I wouldn't see her again until late in the evening. Edith never had much money with her that week, and we lived solely on one loaf of bread. Cliff the young son of the owner of the boarding house, used to share his small bag of chips with me every night. I am very sure that mother didn't have a clue of what went on that week. If she had known I cant think what would have happened.

I was a typical "Tomboy" even though I was quiet, extremely sensitive and shy, and preferred to play outside with the local boys. I found their games much more interesting like cricket, and rounders, and also joined in with them when they built carts out of boxes and old perambulator wheels, mainly getting the job of pushing them around. I thought that girls were silly, dancing and prancing about. I enjoyed skipping and that kind of thing though, which we carried out with old pieces of rope. I always envied the few girls who possessed a real skipping rope with handles, but never got one. Like those children with scooters - how I wanted one of those!! We learned to make our own toys out of cardboard boxes, or in fact anything which we found and thought useful. Now and then, particularly Christmas time, mother did manage to afford one or two small toys to give us, and also to fill our black stockings hanging over the fireplace with a new penny, a few sweets, nuts, and piece of fruit, that was an exciting time. I recall one year getting a parcel of goodies from "Uncle Mac" of the children's radio programme, it was wonderful, we never knew where he got our names and address from, but were very glad that he did. Also to make sure that we had a Christmas dinner mother would go to a butcher's shop late on Christmas Eve and wait for the butcher to auction off very cheaply the chickens that were unsold, and which he was unable to keep fresh over the holiday. We gathered chestnuts from the trees and played "conkers" with the other children, "hopscotch" with pebbles on the pavement, got a few marbles or found cigarette-cards to exchange or play with. We never found time to be bored. There was a game which did not find favour with parents called "knocking down ginger", (don't ask me why), where all the children would gather together at dusk, then one would run and knock at someone's front door while the others hid, he or she would then run away , finding a great deal of amusement when the house owner answered the door to find nobody there. Well, it was highly amusing and great fun to us children at the time, although it sounds strange now. The local boys were regular 'tearaways' at times. Once a number of them waited outside my front gate and asked me to go with them and keep watch. I had no idea what I had to watch out for, and stood outside a Vicarage garden while they all disappeared over the fence. Suddenly there was quite a commotion and exodus by the boys, leaving me to face a rather angry Vicar. He asked me my name and address, and being me of course I had no hesitation giving it to him before leaving to go home. Several days later I was helping my mother by endeavouring to turn the handle of the huge mangle for her, when the Vicar called. He told her that one of her children had been involved in stealing apples from his trees. She shook her head and said it couldn't be, as she had no small boys. Looking past her he pointed to me and said , "that's the one". After apologising to him and closing the front door, mother turned around and looked at me. I waited for the explosion but to my amazement she roared with laughter, and thought it was very funny. Thank goodness,- but I told her later that I hadn't even seen as much as an apple, and she just laughed.

When the living room fire was alight we also made toast by holding a long wire toasting fork in front of it. I can remember Edith and Elsie trying to curl their hair by putting the old iron fire tongs into the red hot coals to heat, then cooling them a little, and winding strands of their hair around them. The smell of burnt hair was terrible, but they always appeared to be satisfied with the result. (Mother used to have very long hair which hung right down her back, and when she had five minutes free to sit down ,she allowed Edith and Elsie to brush it as much as they liked. I remember when I was quite young that I accompanied her to a hairdressers and cried bitterly when she had it all cut off to wear it short. The hairdresser asked Mother if she wanted to keep the shorn off tresses, sell them, or could they just keep them. She said they could have them if they wanted, or throw them away.)

We never had any new clothes to wear, just "hand-me-downs" from one child or person to the next, or mother would manage to re-make clothes for us out of old discarded ones. Because I was always falling sick with heavy colds or flu, she made me wear a type of short-legged combinations which I hated, and which I found extremely embarrassing when having to change for P.T. at school. (I remember later, when at Senior school we had to wear a type of uniform i.e., a gym-slip and white blouse, she made me up a navy-blue gym-slip which although she had worked hard doing it, always looked a little odd against the ones the other girls wore making me feel terribly self-conscious, although I knew that she had done her best. It was during my time in Senior School that I was first told that I suffered from an Inferiority Complex.) Mother often told me about a cream trouser suit she had managed to make for my eldest half-brother George when he was a boy, and how, the first time he wore it he climbed through a large number of huge drainpipes lying around where the builders had been, coming out covered from head to foot in rust, thus ruining it completely. An incident she never forgot! I recall that we never had gloves or mittens to wear in the winter months and my hands were always frozen and the fingers covered with chilblains. Our shoes were also "hand-me-downs" and difficult to wear, and my feet and toes were also blessed with chilblains in the cold weather.

When any one of us children weren't well, mother would doctor us up herself. There were delicious doses of Quinine, or Sulphur Powder poured down into the throat while the victim was bodily held by someone, or of course Castor Oil. Then, and I wore them more than anyone, Brown Paper Vests coated with thick greasy Tallow, and a small square of Camphor hanging on a string around the neck like some kind of decoration. We never visited the Dentist, it was too costly, and when there was a problem with a tooth, (mainly a loose one), a string was tied to the door handle of the room, the other to the tooth, someone would hold the victim tightly while somebody else banged the door shut. Thus removing the offensive item. There was an occasion when Bella cut Edith's hair, and in doing so accidentally cut a small piece of her ear-lobe off as well. Mother sent everyone into the garden shed to look for cobwebs, and stuck the missing piece of ear-lobe back on with one. It was fine and worked well.

My sister Elsie and brother Fred always went to a school kitchen where they served free dinners for the poor. They took me along with them one lunchtime when I was considered to be old enough, and I thought it was terrible there. The food wasn't bad I suppose, but the place was crowded and so noisy, like Bedlam. I was terrified, and refused to go back, so continued to return home for lunch which, as it was usually weak watery Stew containing Onions, which I hated and still do, I just couldn't eat. I remember mother saying "You will sit there and eat it, even if you're late back to school", but I never did. I simply ate the dry bread.

I was of course a skinny little kid, and recall the Head teacher often feeding me Horlick's tablets and taking me inside the Staff Room to sit by the roaring fire. (Children who were considered to be undernourished in those days were also given spoonfuls of Cod Liver Oil and Malt, which I loved,. 'Parishes' Food, and about 1/3rd fresh milk to drink.)Elsie and Fred also took me with them one day to a Park with a swimming pool. This being my first time and not being able to swim, when I was pushed off the side into the water by a boy, and then my legs grabbed and pulled from under me by other boys half drowning me, I never went again. I would love to be able to swim, but that experience did it. Another time I recall going out with Elsie and Fred to see what we could buy for Christmas with a penny from Woolworths. It was quite a long walk and rather misty. We went all around the store, I can't remember buying anything, but when we came out it was thick fog, a real 'pea- souper'. We couldn't see a thing and ended up taking the wrong road home. It seemed to be an endless road but at least we were going in the right direction. It was a side road but we were overtaken I remember by a London Bus crawling along and being asked by the driver where he could find the main road. It was almost impossible to see anything. The fogs in those days were terrible. We did get home eventually. Years later the fogs became smogs. These were absolutely black, and to stop them the Government banned ordinary coal fires and we had to have smokeless fuel, which of course was very expensive.

I don't know if my brother Fred ever remembers it but I do. The time when I was very small and he gave me a razor blade to play with. I cut the top of my finger nearly off and mother had to rush me to a local clinic for it to be stitched back on. I never told her about the razor blade because he'd begged me not to, and to say that Id cut it with a bit of wire fencing. She never questioned me again about it. Another time on Guy Fawkes night, Fred and his friend Jimmy gave me a firework "banger" to hold assuring me that it was alright, just a Sparkler. Of course when it exploded my hand was very painful and I cried my eyes out. A good thing it was one of the old cheap ones, unlike the ones they sell in this day and age or I would have been minus a finger or two! I also recall hearing Fred and Jimmy in the back bedroom and walking in to see them both gazing out of the open window holding an Air-gun and focusing it on a boy along the road who was digging his back garden. I can't remember who it was that fired the shot but the aim was perfect as it hit the boy in the rear and he let out such a yell. Both Fred and Jimmy rushed out of the bedroom nearly knocking me over and also out of the house and were off on their bicycles, before a very irate bad tempered father came around shouting and raving at poor mother who knew nothing about the incident. I didn't say a word.

Every Sunday, when the weather wasn't too bad, mother would collect us all together and take us for a long walk into Hainault Forest for the day. I don't know how many miles we had to cover, but it was quite a distance, and we usually got there just after lunchtime. Edith invited one of her boyfriends to accompany us one day, and I recall him collapsing and sitting down on the pavement half way there, unable to go any further. When we reached the beautiful forest we used to climb trees, collect Crab-apples, and Blackberries if they were in season, and thoroughly enjoy ourselves, walking home in the late afternoon, or evening. We loved it. Mother used to make Crab-apple Jelly, and stew the Blackberries. Strange to say we never felt tired after the long trek home just very happy.

I used to love reading comics as well as books, and these had to be borrowed from the other children in the street because we couldn't afford to buy them ourselves. I was going home and passing a neighbour's house when I was only about eight or nine years old, and was stopped by her teenage "spotty", rather obnoxious son. He told me he had a lot of comics indoors that I could have and ushered me into the house. There was no one else in, and I didn't see any comics. He then forced me to the floor and raped me. I had no idea what he was doing, but screamed my head off to no avail, to which he repeatedly said, no one would hear me and they didn't. When I eventually escaped I ran home badly frightened, shaken and upset. No one was in. I did not know what had really happened, or what it was all about but inwardly knew it was very wrong. I was too afraid to tell my mother or anyone when they came home, and until now never did. I had no idea about the facts of life, sex or anything , this was never discussed by my mother or teachers, and in fact never was, even when I grew older. (If we ever asked mother where babies came from, she would always say "from under the Gooseberry bush")

One Sunday, just after lunch in September 1939, when I was almost ten years old, we were listening to the wireless when Mr. Chamberlain declared war on Germany because of the invasion of Poland. I did not really understand what was happening, but my poor mother did, having already lived through one world war. She clearly remembered all the suffering and the bombings by the German Zeppelins, not to mention her beloved first husband dying in the trenches in France.

Within a very short period of time everyone was allocated with Identity Cards, Ration Books, and of course Gas Masks. Deep holes were dug at the bottom of gardens and corrugated Anderson shelters were installed. These shelters were well covered with piles of earth. They simply contained four iron-webbed bunk beds. One of the main problems with them was that they were so damp inside, nothing, mattresses or bed-linen etc., could be used, and all anyone of us, in an air-raid could do was lie on the iron-webbing which was most uncomfortable, and did not encourage sleep. There was always a considerable amount of water also lying at the bottom which seeped up through the dirt floor, through which one had to paddle upon entering. However, we were extremely glad of these shelters during the heavy and persistent air-raids.

One morning, without telling me where we were going, my mother placed the small cardboard box containing my Gas Mask on a string around my neck, handed me a carrier bag and took me on a bus to London. There, on a Thames river dock with hundreds of other children about my age, she kissed me goodbye and I was taken by a teacher with the others on board a large paddle-steamer to be evacuated.

Chapter two:

As a ten year old child who had never spent any time at all at the sea-side or in the country, I was of course just a "'Townie". Now suddenly I was in the wilds of rural Essex, surrounded by fields of vegetables, huge trees, orchards and farm yards. I was in the midst of laughing, shouting village children. Climbing trees and uprooting large turnips from the fields to eat them raw. Walking three and a half miles across the fields to the tiny village school four times a day with my "Townie" friend. Sleeping in the big double bed with my friend in the back room of the row of half a dozen council houses.

It was all very wonderful. On the way home from school every afternoon we would each steal an apple from the overhanging branches of the giant tree in the farm-yard, hiding them in the elasticated legs of our navy-blue knickers until we were safely away, then consuming them voraciously. We also discovered that we were able to help ourselves from the collections of bruised fallen apples which were placed on the top of the hedgerows. It was certainly very different to life in suburbia, and the monotonous rows of regimental council houses, where nothing was freely given away, and the only fresh air was marred by the smell of smoke and melting tarmac on the roads.

It seemed like only yesterday that I was standing alone in part of the village school playground. All the other evacuees had been chosen by the voluntary foster parents, leaving me standing feeling lost and unwanted. My friend quickly came to my rescue and refused to leave unless the couple who had chosen her, took me along as well. Which although none too happy about it, they did. They already had one child of their own. A little girl of about nine, and had only been prepared to accept one evacuee. We both tried hard to make friends with their little girl, but she resented our presence, having always been the only child. I remember feeling very sorry for her because she had an ear complaint. Both her ears being continually stuffed with messy discoloured cotton wool. She clung closely to her rather cold natured parents who were very quiet and undemonstrative. The grandfather kept ferrets. I'd never seen these strange creatures before and was amazed by their suppleness, white colour and pink eyes. Warning me about their sharp teeth, the grandfather allowed me to stroke them and told me how he used them to catch the rabbits which we ate so frequently for our meals. I wasn't too happy about this as it seemed to be very unkind, not to mention cruel, to the poor rabbits.

The journey to Brantham had in itself been both exciting and a little disconcerting. We'd left London by Paddle Steamer clutching our suitcases and with our Gas Masks hanging around our necks on a piece of string. The carrier bag that we'd been given contained sandwiches and to my surprise and astonishment, a giant bar of chocolate. I'd never seen so much chocolate and could hardly believe it. I treasured it all the way there, convinced that someone would ask for it back, if I dared eat it. The trip down the river Thames was a lot of fun. I ran around the deck and from side to side, watching the huge paddles churning up the water and fascinated by everything I saw. It was late in the evening when we arrived at Clacton and discovered that there were no coaches available for our onward journey.

We stood wearily for what appeared to be ages on the end of the Pier while our accompanying teachers argued with a number of official looking people, before boarding a bus which took us to a local school. There we spent a long sleepless night in the school hall bedded down on a lightly sprinkled straw covered floor. I recall that we were given two thin single blankets between three children, one to lie on and one supposedly to cover us. Supposedly was right! In the morning we were given a drink and ate the rest of our sandwiches before boarding a coach, which took us to the village school in Brantham. A crowd of 'fostering parents' had already gathered in the playground, and we climbed down and stood waiting to be' chosen '. It wasn't a particularly nice feeling, especially amongst so many strangers.

Although very quiet and rather timid, I quickly made friends with the local children, and as I was a 'Tom-boy', played as usual with the boys enjoying their games. I recall finding an old car tyre in a ditch one day and was happily bowling it along the country lane on the way home from the village shop about two miles away, clutching a half-eaten toffee bar in my other hand. Suddenly to my surprise a bicycle appeared around the corner bearing my portly, dignified, well dressed headmistress. I could have died on the spot! She stopped pedalling, dismounted and frowned down on me most displeased. How terribly embarrassed and ridiculous I felt with that tyre. "Why aren't you at school?" she demanded. I explained somehow or other that I understood that as we shared the school half-day with the village children, the afternoons were our own. "Nonsense," she replied, "It's to be lessons in the mornings and the teachers are taking you on rambles in the afternoons. Make sure that you are at school tomorrow, all day." She remounted her bicycle and elegantly rode off, leaving me standing there duly chastened. From that day on I dutifully attended school every afternoon and was taken on interesting rambles around the surrounding countryside.

The school was very small and rather quaint from a 'Townie's' point of view, but inside quite cosy in comparison with the ones I was used to. One morning the teacher asked me to go outside into the hall and see what the time was by the big clock. I felt very embarrassed as I had never been taught how to tell the time, and therefore hadn't got a clue. I couldn't admit this somehow as I felt too ashamed. I went outside and gazed helplessly at the clock face for sometime before returning to the classroom and mumbling "I think it's gone twelve o'clock." My teacher looked at me but never commented. My friend quickly realized my problem and later when we were in the bedroom at home, spent a lot of time drawing clock faces and trying to teach me how to tell the time. I just couldn't understand her somehow, and it was later at my own home that my dear mother showed me by the clock on the mantlepiece. It seemed quite simple once she had explained. As a 'latch key' kid and because mother was a busy working widow, there hadn't been much time to teach me things like 'telling the time'. I and no one else in the family possessed a watch. That was a luxury we could never have afforded.

Apart from the minor embarrassments and missing my mother, I quite enjoyed the short time I spent in Brantham. The countryside was wonderful. It was a different world, and the local children were so friendly. My mother however, visited me one Sunday morning at about eleven o'clock and was disgusted to find that everyone was still in bed, and that the old tin bath used by all of us the previous night, was still standing in front of the living room fireplace containing the dirty bath water. She of course had strong words about this with my 'foster parents' before she left. Mother wasn't at all happy about the way we were being looked after either. A few days later I received a letter from her telling me to be on the Saturday night coach home, and that she'd meet me at the other end of the journey. She had discussed the matter with my friend's mother and she was also displeased, and was arranging for her to return home, but not on the same coach as it was full.

When I boarded the coach as instructed, the only vacant seat was at the back in the middle of the long bench seat between two very large ladies. I perched there precariously in silence. As we sped along in the pitch darkness the coach swerved at a corner and went down into a ditch, sending me sprawling the whole length of the vehicle. Apart from shock and a few bruises, luckily I was unhurt. Everyone had to get out and it took hours with the help of farm hands using wooden planks and working by torchlight, to get the front wheels out of the ditch and back onto the road. We were therefore very late arriving at our destination, and mother who was still waiting for me was extremely worried.

I wasn't allowed to remain at home however, because of the air-raids, and mother quickly packed me off with my sister Elsie to live with my half-brother Alec, his wife and two small children, in March,Cambridgeshire.It wasn't so nice there as Brantham as it was a railway marshalling town, and I hated it. Alec worked as a Shunter on the railway and was therefore in a reserved occupation. Alec had brown hair, was quiet, firm, and very shrewd, but was kind hearted and had a sense of humour. I was terrified of Alec however, who although not a bit violent in any way whatsoever, had a sharp voice and a forbidding look. Elsie who was fourteen went to work on the land, and I was enrolled at another school. I didn't know a soul, and everyone there was very unfriendly. They appeared to look down on me because I was a Londoner, and it was quite a posh school. They even played Hockey. They'd never played such games at any of my local schools, just the usual netball and rounders. The teacher asked me superciliously one day what letters were on my exercise books at home, was it E.C.C. or L.C.C. I couldn't remember at all, and all the children in the class were looking in my direction. Because my home address was Essex, I thought it must be E.C.C. and confidently said so, but I'd got it wrong. "You're a liar." the teacher shouted almost gleefully, and the whole class laughed. I felt so humiliated. I'd never been called a liar before and it hurt so. I wasn't at all happy at the school, never made a single friend and was very lonely. All I wanted was to go home.

On my way home from school every day I used to stand on top of the iron bridge over the railway lines at the level-crossing, and look down on the empty trucks chugging along below. So tempted was I to jump down into one and go home, but unfortunately I had no idea in which direction London lay. I was often late home from school because of this, and later would hear my sister-in-law complaining to Alec about this and also about the soot and grime on my clothes from the railway. I was so terribly lonely and homesick. The only friend I made in the town was the Baker's rounds man who let me take the reigns and drive his horse and cart whenever he came with the bread. I really loved that horse.

I was given the job of washing-up the dishes every night after the main meal and Alec gave me sixpence a week for this task. The kitchen stood apart from the main building, separated by a small hallway and the back door, and was rather isolated. I was very nervous out there on my own at night up to my elbows in soapsuds and dishes. From the shut off living room I could just hear the family chatter and laughter as I worked. I was so alone and was always afraid that an intruder would come through the back door whilst I was helpless, and that no one would hear me if I cried out. My imagination played havoc. It wasn't so bad in the summertime when the nights were still light. I recall looking up from the sink one evening to see mother's dear face smiling at me through the window. I nearly dropped a plate with surprise as I rushed to the door to greet her, my hands and arms covered in soapsuds. She visited us several times and I always begged her to take me home.

Another terrible night time ordeal was visiting the outside toilet by torchlight. I was a very nervous child and was terrified. Especially if I had to go out there in the middle of the night when everyone was asleep. Elsie admitted later that she had hated it too.

In addition to her work on the land, Elsie took on a part-time job in a local sweet shop. The owner was very friendly with my sister-in-law, and used to send Elsie home with sweets and chocolates for the babies. Elsie and I rarely got any for ourselves. One evening as we were going for a walk, Elsie produced at least twelve small bars of chocolate, handed six to me and said "Let's you and I eat these for a change." I of course was only too willing. After gorging ourselves we returned home where I was up all night being sick and ill. We didn't dare say that we had been stuffing ourselves with chocolate, so Alec called the doctor, and I was off from school for a couple of days with 'an upset stomach'. Elsie and I laughed about it later.

One Saturday, Alec had the brilliant idea of sending me out into the fields with Elsie potato picking, to earn a little money. At that age I was so afraid of him I had no say in the matter. I had nothing suitable to wear for such an   occasion so he sorted through his own wardrobe and found some of his old clothes for me to wear. He dressed me up in a pair of old baggy trousers which were of course far too big for me, a torn jacket also too large, even with the sleeves rolled up out of the way, and worse than that a pair of his heavy hob-nailed boots in which my small feet slipped up and down, and were so heavy I could barely lift them off the ground. I'm sure that I must have looked, as I felt, like a 'Pint sized Scarecrow'. I was thus despatched with Elsie at the crack of dawn. What anyone must have thought at the sight of me I shudder to think. It wasn't long before I was limping along, badly crippled by the heavy boots, and attempting to negotiate a ploughed field carrying a heavy bucket in which to put the potatoes I collected, if any. We were told to follow a large rather antiquated tractor and Elsie advised me to try to stay close to her so that she could look after me. Not that I recall seeing much of her once the tractor started off with a great roar and splutter. It turned over the earth as it proceeded and we all followed in a long straggling line, our bodies bent over, struggling to collect the exposed potatoes and put them into our buckets. In a very short time my back ached abominably, apart from the pain coming from my poor ill-treated feet as Alec's boots rubbed them raw. I was soon left far behind the others, and simply picked up any stray potatoes I could find. I struggled onwards, ever onwards, and don't know how I managed to last the day out. I do know however, how I felt afterwards. Every bone and muscle in my body throbbed endlessly. I had never realized that there were so many places anyone could hurt at one and the same time. Back at home my poor bleeding and raw feet had to be bathed and bandaged, and would only accept a pair of old, four sizes too large, plimsolls. My aches and pains lasted a week and even stepping up a curb was excruciating. I think that my earned money only amounted to less than a shilling, and Alec was disgusted. I decided then and there that outdoor farm and field work was not for me, and that Elsie could have it!

My sister-in-law's mother also lived in March. She had a

converted railway carriage for a home. It was very cosy and comfortable. There were quite a few of these homes in the town. I really enjoyed visiting her. She was about my mother's age and I got on very well with her. I used to call on her as often as I could, always on my own. She had a delightful budgerigar, and loved animals as much as I did. I always thought of her as a good friend.

In Alec's bungalow, where Elsie and I were staying, the full kettle was always kept boiling on the open fireplace. One day, while my sister-in-law was bathing the babies in front of the fire, Elsie reached over and took hold of the kettle handle without the protecting cloth. It was of course red hot, and with a loud cry she dropped it. The boiling water went everywhere and all down her leg. The babies both screamed with fright, and poor Elsie was screaming with pain. It was pandemonium. Alec and his wife quickly turned to the babies thinking that they had been hurt, and I ran to help Elsie, who was hopping around the room in agony before collapsing on to a chair. Finding that the babies weren't harmed at all, Alec then attempted to help Elsie but did not know what to do. She was crying, and I was also crying because she was in so much pain. Alec gave me some money and sent me to a little shop some distance away to see if they had something to put on Elsie's leg to help. I ran and cried all the way there, told the woman what had happened, but she hadn't a clue what to give me, then finally she gave me a bottle of mixture which I gave to Alec. He dabbed it onto Elsie's leg but she screamed even louder, so he sent for the doctor and he sorted it out. Elsie was off work for over a week and in an awful lot of pain. I was terribly upset about her suffering, and can still remember it all vividly.

I spent a lot of my spare time helping my sister-in-law with the housework, polishing, and cleaning, and quite enjoyed doing it. My half-sister Bella visited us one day and when she returned home told mother that she thought I was being turned into a 'drudge', so mother immediately sent Alec the train fare to send me home. I was thrilled, but Alec didn't want to lose the evacuation allowance he was getting for me. As he got free train fare for himself and family by working on the railway, and he was angry about Bella's story, he dressed Elsie up as his wife and they went home to see mother and tell her that there was nothing at all to worry about, I was fine and being well looked after. Mother couldn't have been completely happy about this however, as a few week's later she sent Fred who was on leave fom the Merchant Navy, to fetch me home. What utter bliss. To be going home at last. I recall sitting in the railway carriage opposite my handsome brother, who looked dashing in his Navy uniform with it's gold buttons and peaked cap also well adorned with gold trimmings and Merchant Navy badge. To me then he was like a Prince from a Fairy Tale. (I never dared tell him this of course). Fred had auburn hair, was tall, kindhearted with a good sense of humour which sometimes develolped into devilment. When we got home I discovered mother in bed with influenza and was glad to be there so I could be of some help to her. When she was better I returned to my old school where to my surprise I found my evacuee friends and teachers, who for some undisclosed reasons, had decided to return to London war or no war, and suffer the terrible blitz.

Chapter 3

It was wonderful to be home again with my mother and family, that is those who were not away in the forces at this time, or evacuated into the country , which left only two or three. George I remember was in the Mercantile Marines, Bella's husband Jim the Navy, Fred as I mentioned was in the Merchant Navy, (He had been at sea since shortly after leaving school at fourteen starting as a "Bell Boy", and then later being promoted to a Steward on the large Ocean Liners, before joining the Merchant Navy.) Edith was working in a local munitions factory as an Inspector in the manufacture of Aeroplanes. (The factory had previously been used to manufacture car bodies.)

Elsie came home from Alec's and found a job in the city until she became old enough to join the Women's LandArmy, thus getting back to her belove'd open-air farm work. Mother now in addition to all her other tasks had found work cleaning in the local schools, which was extremely like hard labour in those days having to move all the heavy old-fashioned desks, and scrub the wooden floors. I used to go along after school and during the summer holidays to help her. I remember spending a great deal of time washing up lots of plastic cups and beakers which the pupils had used as well, which she was expected to do, before helping her to move the desks and so on. I just loved being able to help her in any way I could. (I must admit though as a child I was always a little envious of the children who went home from school to a warm welcome and a nourishing tea laid on by their mothers, who never had to go out to work like mine.)

There was much more employment available during the war and things improved somewhat money-wise. We were on rations for food, clothes, and sweets, and there wasn't much fruit and imported products available, it seemed however, that life was a little easier for us. We were very glad of the Marshal Plan which improved the rationing in some ways. The bringing in of Dried Eggs, which we loved, (I couldn't get enough of it and would love to have it now in preference to fresh eggs), also Dried Milk. Whale meat we fought shy of, didn't fancy it at all, we did eat a lot of Spam however. The queues for food of any kind were dreadful. Because of the clothes rationing women were unable to afford precious coupons for stockings so went without, or used Gravy Browning to colour their legs. When the Americans joined in the war the Yanks all managed to provide their English girlfriends with Nylon stockings, much to the disgust of our own uniformed forces, who were unable to compete. The government encouraged everyone to grow and produce their own food as far as possible, so we did. We also began to keep chickens, ducks and a few rabbits. All the local Parks had their lawns removed and grew vegetables in their place. (I remember that we were never allowed on the park lawns when they were there anyway, and the numerous Park Keepers made sure of this. There were also large signs 'Keep off the grass' as well.) I noticed that all the iron railings everywhere, even gates, had been dismantled and taken away for the manufacture of munitions. In the Park at the top of our road there was a gun emplacement which made a terrible noise during the air-raids, as the guns fired on the enemy aircraft weaving their way through the accumulation of large Barrage

Balloons floating in the sky above. There were of course quite a few Search Lights which lit up the night-sky as bright as day, and which with the addition of the gun fire and the menacing throbbing of German planes, quite terrified me, especially when trying to run to the bottom of the garden to the shelter. If there was an air-raid during school time, we had to stay at our desks until the enemy planes were right overhead before we were instructed to hurry in an orderly fashion into a brick built shelter in the playground.

Edith, who at about seventeen, had quarrelled quite violently with mother because of keeping late hours seeing her many boyfriends, and who, in front of us all, had attempted to strike mother with a sauce bottle from the dinner table, left home to live as a boarder in an Irish immigrant part of the district, near her factory. (Edith was very dark, had some big ideas, and was rather ostentatious, she also spent a lot of time reading love stories, which mother was convinced led her astray.)   It was several months later however, that mother received a letter from the landlady of the boarding house in which Edith was staying , telling her that she no longer wanted Edith there because of her many men friends calling. Mother of course made haste and went to bring her home again.

Once she was home it was discovered that she was pregnant, and when questioned, had no idea who the man involved was. I recall accompanying mother and Edith to a house in Romford where they took in single pregnant women, but when mother discovered all the rough work the women were expected to do whilst awaiting the birth, she brought Edith home and cared for her there. (Even then when all this was going on I still hadn't got a clue about the "facts of life"). Edith continued working at the munitions factory as long as she could. Then, Elsie was awoken by mother early one morning and sent along for the doctor, who came immediately and who was assisted by mother, until Edith gave birth to a baby girl in the front bedroom. Putting the baby into a cot, mother noticed its eyes full of yellow puss and pointed this out to the doctor who hurriedly sent for an ambulance. Apparently Edith had unfortunately contracted Syphilis and without prompt attention the baby could have gone blind. In due time when the baby, named Margaret, was a few months old Edith returned to her job at the factory, and I was given the undesirable task of taking Margaret to a nursery about twenty minutes away before attending school every morning.

In doing so I had to pass the Senior boy's school playground where I remember being subjected to numerous loud 'cat calls' which I hated and did not understand. I did know however, that upon entering Senior school at the age of eleven, I found that I no longer quite liked the boys of that age, I don't know why, but never played with or amongst them anymore. (Schools at that time were quite separate for boys and girls.) My friends now were girls of my own age. The mother of one of these girls gave me one shilling and six pence a week for running errands for her. These errands were only for small items but she wanted them carried out at least four times a day for some reason or other. I never understood why they could not all be bought at the same time, or why her own young daughter did not run the errands for her, but I was glad to earn the money so never enquired.

Fred always brought a large kit-bag with him when he came home on leave full of his dirty washing for mother to do. She never complained, but even as children we all hated 'washing day' and used to sing the childish 'ditty', "Rain, rain go away, come back on washing day'," hoping that it would be put off because it would be impossible to dry the clothes. It was a miserable day for everyone, and such a terribly hard task for mother to perform in those days.

The fire under the copper had to be lit and kept well stoked to boil the sheets and whites, and for enough hot water to fill the kitchen sink. Then each item washed by rubbing it on the heavy glass-ribbed scrubbing board accompanied by a large bar of Sunlight soap, until clean. After rinsing, the laundry would then have to be put singly through the rollers of the giant mangle before hanging it outdoors on the clothes line to dry. Ironing was also a hard tiresome job. The 'flat' irons had to be heated on the living room fire one at a time, then wiped clean before use and finally returned to the fire for reheating. I often recall the happy day Elsie returned home from work and presented mother with her first Electric iron. It made such a great difference. Mother was thrilled and we were all delighted.

When Elsie was fifteen she was given Edith's racing type bicycle, so gave me the one mother had surprised her with at the age of fourteen, by sending her on a 'so called' errand to the cycle shop where the manager told her to choose and take the bicycle she liked. (Apparently mother had been secretly paying off for it for sometime.) I was so pleased to get Elsie's bicycle and loved it, and from then on rode it everywhere, eventually to and from work. Elsie also came home one day and presented me with a pair of Roller Skates for my birthday. I was overjoyed, but after trying them out discovered that they would not work properly because there were no ball-bearings in them. I was so very upset and disappointed that mother raised enough money to buy me a better pair. Now what with the bicycle and the skates, I was overwhelmed, and suddenly very mobile. Elsie also bought me my very first Dictionary together with several books from her pocket-money now that she was working. She was always good to me and thinking of me - 'her little sister'.

I was thirteen when I first experienced 'the curse'. I had no idea what had or was happening to me again, Elsie was the one who gave me an 'S.T.' and showed me how to use it. No explanation or information was forthcoming from either her or my mother, or the fact that this event would occur every month. I was left completely in the dark as usual. (These matters were not discussed in my family, or in fact amongst any of my friends. It appeared to me to be a very 'Taboo' and secretive matter. One not to be enquired about, so I didn't.) Unfortunately I suffered greatly with the curse every month, the pains were almost unbearable and hard to treat even with strong painkillers and using really hot water bottles held against my stomach. I even drank no end of hot peppermint, to no avail. Sickness also accompanied the stomach ache. I was really ill every month. Later, when at work, I usually had to give in and stagger over to the First Aid Department where nine times out of ten the doctor sent me home by ambulance. It was most embarrassing. I felt as if the whole world knew about it, even the neighbours. Was I glad when later in life it disappeared for good!!

It was also about this age (thirteen) when mother took me aside and told me that her second husband was not my father, gave me a photograph of my real father and told me his name, which was Edward Rogers. Apparently he lodged with her, they fell in love and I was the result. He worked on a local building site. Mother said that when I was born he was delighted and bought me some nice baby clothes. After a while though they had a disagreement and parted. This affair took place while her second husband was still in the Asylum. I was not at all bothered at being illegitimate, just extremely grateful that she had not put me up for adoption or into a Home, and loved her all the more for keeping me.

The war was still raging and we spent every night in the shelter listening to the bombs raining down and the Anti Aircraft guns firing. We followed the news on the wireless and in the newspapers, and listened and was duly fortified by Winston Churchill's wonderful rhetoric. He certainly did everything he could to raise the people's morale and strengthen their courage, and thus carried everyone through. Shortly after an air-raid one afternoon I was standing in the garden looking up at the sky when I thought I could see in the distance, something resembling a full-moon. I stood there and watched as this small object gradually grew larger and larger, until I recognised that it was a parachute.

Then a man along the road a few houses away who was in his garden, gave a loud shout which was followed by many more shouts and cries from other men. I continued to watch and eventually saw the figure of a person clinging to the ropes of the parachute and swaying to and fro as it descended. Suddenly more shouts came from all around and panic appeared to break out amongst all the neighbouring men whom I believe were mostly Home Guards. Then a shot was fired, followed by many more. I could then see the figure quickly attempting to raise up it's legs again and again, in what appeared to me to be futile moves to avoid the flying bullets. I was very upset as I watched to know that the men were firing on a helpless person, whoever it was. I could do or say nothing. I heard later that the parachutist had descended in a local street and had thereupon been mobbed and killed. It was only afterwards that everyone discovered that the man was not a German as suspected, but an English flyer, one of 'our own boys'. It had been a terrible mistake, but of course it was quickly hushed up.

Mother had a few days off from work, and on one of these took me by coach to visit her sisters, one in Gloucester and the eldest in Cardiff. Her eldest sister Aunt Min., (short for Wilhelmina) although also a very poor widow, always sent mother part of her tea ration, and me some sweets, needless to say both of these items were most welcome. She was very kind hearted, and a dear soul. When we arrived we found that because she was still terrified of Electricity, her small internally badly damaged terraced house was lit entirely by Gas lamps. Most of these were without mantles and flared dangerously. So mother and I set out searching the town everywhere until in an old-fashioned shop we managed to find some, then bought and fitted them for her. I recall that the interior of her house badly needed attention and that even the stair banisters were broken and unsafe. We could do nothing to help her with this problem except to persuade her to complain most strongly to the Landlord. Mother's other living sister Aunt Elsie in Gloucester, was also extremely nice. She was married and quite comfortably off. While in Gloucester I met some of my cousins who were very friendly and were a few years older than me. During this coach trip mother and I noticed many Italian Prisoners of War working in the fields alongside the other civilian farm workers and Land Army girls. To all appearances they seemed to be quite settled and happy, and not in the least dangerous or anxious to escape.

Chapter 4.

I left school at the age of fourteen and after attending an interview during which the Personnel Officer carefully studied my school report, I started work as an office junior in a local Engineering Firm. The hours were 9 am -5.30 pm, and one Saturday morning in four. The salary was only twelve shillings and sixpence a week, but it was a beginning, and I could now learn everything and help mother 'money- wise' at last. (I had always dreamed of becoming a Writer but that was out of the question.) Determined to make upward progress I then began to start work an hour earlier every morning and stay an hour later in the evening, learning how to type by addressing all the secretary's envelopes for her etc.,for which she was extremely happy to give me advice and some guidance. There was all kinds of things to do in the job including filing, and a great deal of running about with messages and papers to various departments. Unfortunately during my first year at work I caught Scarlet Fever, and later on Yellow Jaundice, both from Elsie, so lost quite a lot of time out sick. My boss was then considerably startled and quite surprised when, after a hard time summoning up the courage, I suddenly asked him for a raise in salary! He was so amused by the whole episode that, laughing all the time, he agreed to give me an extra five shillings a week. When I told mother the news she was of course very pleased. (In those days it was customary to give your parents or parent as the case may be, your pay packet to deduct enough money for your keep, then you would be given back some pocket money.) Because of the air-raids I was always worried as I turned the last corner on my way home from work in case I found my house bombed and in ruins, terrified lest mother had been injured etc., the fear was always there.   I then enrolled in a local college for Evening Classes to learn shorthand and typewriting and a foreign language. Strange to say I chose German, did'nt fancy French at all. The college hours were 7 pm.-9 pm. So I could no longer stay later at the office in the evenings.

Some months later, one of my friends told me about a vacancy in a local Chemical Company for an office girl with a slight knowledge of shorthand and typing. The salary being offered was thirty shillings a week, for the same number of hours and it was in an Export Documentation Department. I was told that the Company usually only employed people from Colleges or Grammar Schools, but because of the war staffing problem had had to lower their standards. I applied, went for an interview, and got the job. My present boss Mr.Carling was rather upset at my leaving, but said that he quite understood.

I started my new job and found that, although there was still filing and a lot of running about, there was also a little shorthand dictation and typing. The work was much more interesting altogether. We were dealing with documents appertaining to the export of medical and veterinary medicines and drugs to the British Commonwealth. There were Tenders, orders, invoices, Bills of Lading, Airweigh Bills, Letters of Credit, and so forth. Quite fascinating, well at least to me. My Department Head was a woman and we got on well together. I took dictation from her and typed the letters for her to sign. Unfortunately, the woman Supervisor was not so likeable and did her best to make my life a total misery any way she could. Because of her nasty spiteful treatment I went home every evening in tears. Mother was most understanding and helped me to 'dry my tears', and carry on with the job. However, apparently the Supervisor's treatment of me did not go unnoticed by the Department Head, who called me into her office and advised me to take no notice of her nastiness. She explained that it was a form of bitterness because the Supervisor's husband had recently been killed in the war, and that in time her attitude would change. It never did though, even after some time had passed and she married again. I became hardened to her taunts and took no notice, it was the only way. In carrying messages and documents to various departments within the Company I became wellknown and everyone was very friendly, and did all they could to help me. I also made many friends in the other offices, one girl of my own age Maisie, becoming special. Her father was the head of a local Mission, and of course she was very religious. She had a younger sister who eventually became a Missionary in Africa, and was there at the time of the uprising of the Mau-Mau. Maisie and I used to play tennis in the Company's courts sometimes during the lunch hour, and in time when I had free evenings from Evening Classes, she used to come to the house and take piano lessons with me. These lessons were not very successful however, and didn't last as although we both loved music, we had to give up as our teacher was an itinerant and had to stop the practise. I always cycled to and from work in all weathers every day and enjoyed doing so. (We acted in the same way as in school during an air-raid, and only left the office to go into a brick built shelter when the signal came to say that the enemy planes were overhead.)

Edith was still living at home with her small daughter Margaret and working in the munitions factory. Whilst Edith was at work mother somehow managed to look after Margaret and continue with her own working routine.

Now it seemed that Edith was ready to settle down and was looking for a husband. One or two men she knew from the factory called at the house to see her in the evenings, one of which who she called 'little George', was a hunchback. He was very intelligent, kind and polite. He also attended Evening Classes at the college I went to. He began to call at the house quite often, and spent a great deal of time talking to me and giving me books, and telling me that I was a 'dreamer', and to 'wake up', before life passed me by. Edith I'm afraid, gave him short shrift, and had no time for him. 'Little George' however, did not disappear from the scene very quickly, and somehow or other attached himself to me much to my embarassment, and insisted upon accompanying me to the college whenever I went for my classes. He would always place his arm around my shoulders when walking along the street, and as I was so terribly shy and self-conscious, I was most unhappy about this and would have liked to tell him so but felt so sorry for him that I couldn't be unkind. I was very glad though when he decided not to visit the house anymore, and disappeared from our lives. One evening when mother was busy ploughing her way through a huge pile of ironing, I answered a knock on the door to, as I thought, a strange, chubby, plain little workman wearing spectacles, dressed rather shabbily and wearing bright green Wellingtons. These Wellingtons were so unusual looking I found it hard to take my eyes off them, they fascinated me especially as it wasn't raining and the weather was perfectly fine. The man asked to see Edith, who was at that time ill in bed with influenza. He spoke with a Scottish accent. Leaving him at the front door I went into the living room and told mother, who instructed me to let him in. I had no idea at the time that I was admitting my future brother-in-law, he most certainly didn't look Edith's type of boyfriend. He told mother his name was Peter, and said he would like to see Edith. Mother, who at the time was as I said very busy, and I suspect a little tired of Edith's boyfriends, told him to take a seat. He sat down in the armchair and mother simply continued with her ironing making him wait until she had completely finished, which if I remember took some time. He didn't look at all pleased at being made to wait. However, finally mother went out into the passage and called out at the foot of the stairs telling Edith that she had a visitor and must make herself decent as she was sending him up.

He eventually married Edith and never, like me, forgot that evening when mother had made him sit and wait until she felt ready to give him her attention! I still find the episode very amusing when I think about it. (Personally I never did like Peter very much at all, and am well aware that the feeling was mutual, but as I wasn't the one marrying him, I guess it didn't really matter.) He obviously knew how to handle Edith however, and together with little Margaret they went to live temporarily in a small flat above a fish and chip shop a short distance away.

To my great surprise one morning I received a letter from the college saying that I had been awarded a prize for my work in Commerce and giving me the date to attend the prize giving. The prizes were to be handed out by the Right Honourable R.A. Butler, M.P., and family and friends were invited. When the day came I was so terribly nervous I was shaking. It took a great deal of courage for me to step out onto the platform, and take the prize, which I had requested to be in book-form, from the smiling Mr.Butler who seeing the state I was in laughed and said "You look more as if you are going to the dentist, than to collect a prize." Then commenting upon the books I had chosen, which were Roget's Thesaurus, and The Conscise English Dictionary, etc., suggested that my interest appeared to be more in Writing than Commerce, to which I shyly agreed. He smiled and shook my hand wishing me much success in the future and I hastily withdrew. Mother was very disappointed that she was unable to be in the audience, but my dear Elsie was there to congratulate me and escort me home. Elsie, like Edith was very dark, but was thoughtful and kindhearted, and simply adored children. She always told mother that when she grew up she wanted to have an orphanage of her own.

My eldest half-brother George, who was as previously explained serving in the Mercantile Marines, received word that his baby daughter Dawn had died, and requested Compassionate Leave to be with his wife and young son for the funeral. This was refused, but he received leave a few weeks later to visit his family who had been evacuated to the country at the beginning of the war. When he arrived he discovered that his wife had been 'playing around' and leaving the baby every night with his ten year old son while she went to the Public House to enjoy herself. There was a huge row and he left her, bringing his son with him to our house for mother to look after, which she did. The boy, my nephew John, was enrolled at the nearby Grammar School and whenever George obtained leave he also stayed with us. I remember that John had to wear a uniform to school complete with one of those very short Caps on his head, which during the winter months was most inadequate. His ears were always frozen and became badly chapped. Like most boys, he hated washing, and when his father was there he used to grab hold of him and scrub his poor ears that to me looked so sore. John used to yell and struggle, and I felt so sorry for him. Strange the things that stay in your mind!

Elsie left home and joined the Woman's Land Army for her war effort when she was eighteen. She was sent to Stansted in Essex and lodged in a hostel with the other W.L.A. girls stationed there. She loved the work, being back in the fields and farms, but was not too happy about the woman in charge of the hostel, who she claimed was very mean with the food and not at all kind in other ways. Elsie made many friends there however, and used to come home quite often on weekend leave. One Saturday I remember she brought two girl friends with her and they dressed me up in one of her spare uniforms, which consisted of fawn britches, a green pullover and fawn hat, and took me with them to the local Cinema. As I was still very thin and gangly I didn't look a bit like a Land Army Girl, but we all had a good laugh. There was an American Airforce Station at the Aerodrome near where Elsie and the other girls were and they,the girls and the Yanks used to get together at dances and so on during their spare time. I was invited to one of these dances/parties at Christmas time by Elsie and her friends and I went along but soon wished that I hadn't. I am not and never have been a party person although I've tried very hard to join in, I can't dance and am, even now, too shy and selfconscious to start. I was also very shocked at the amount of 'snogging' that went on between the couples on the dance floor, which was of course put down to the existence of Miselto hanging from the ceiling, and I was glad to go home when the party was over. I was and still am the one who always sits in the corner watching everyone enjoying themselves, unable to join in, and also hiding in the background when and if a group photograph was taken. No self- confidence at all. No one had ever told me that I wasn't bad looking or that I was perhaps a little pretty to boost my confidence. So I carried on always feeling that I was the 'ugly duckling' of the family, if not the stupid one. I also think that something went wrong with my Gender too when I was born. I'm not a bit feminine, hate make-up, high heeled shoes and all the feminine attributes, - should have been a boy I'm sure. Something definitely went wrong,I've also always had an allergy to noise and crowds and prefer peace and quiet above all things. I recall mentioning the noise problem to Dr. Dean once when we were chatting and he smiled and said "I'm afraid it's a very noisy world we live in now."

One weekend Elsie brought one of the Yanks home with her. He was very polite, dark haired, serious and quiet, saying very little. Mother made him welcome but quite quickly advised Elsie to have nothing more to do with him as he was married. Elsie was amazed as we all were at this statement, but somehow or other mother was inclined to sum up people or situations very quickly and accurately, we never knew how, but she was always right. Elsie did as she said and never saw him again. It was several months later that Elsie met Bob and brought him home with her for a weekend visit. He was a PFC in the American Eighth Airforce stationed at Stansted, and worked on the ground staff at the Aerodrome. We all took to him immediately, he had such a wonderful boyish personality and was so cheerfully good natured and kind hearted as well as very good looking. His hometown in America was Plymouth, Massachusettes and he was twenty-one. From then on he accompanied Elsie on her home weekend visits, sometimes bringing his best friend Teddy with him who was also very nice. Bob always treated me like his own little sister and when he took Elsie out to the cinema or even into London's West End for the evening he also took me along. As I had never before been to the West End it was wonderful and even with the war on we always had a great time. I soon grew to love him, and looked forward to his visits. These always started off with Bob unzipping his uniform jacket and taking out large tins of peaches etc., and if Teddy was with him he did the same, they laughingly said that they had visited the KP store before leaving the base, knowing that we would all enjoy them. On his visits Bob taught me many things like how best to defend myself, a little Judo, and never to go out on a date without my "mad money". One Judo act that he showed me was to throw him over my shoulder, so I did, and he landed in the flower bed amongst the Chrysanthemums, and Elsie who saw me do it shouted from the upstairs bedroom window "You leave my Bob alone." He was great fun. I remember him telling me how surprised he and all his friends were that in Britain all the shops were closed on Sundays, also on Good Fridays. Also that the beer wasn't chilled like it was in America. Bob came from a family of four, three boys and one girl, and was of French descent although it wasn't noticeable, that is except by his surname and the fact that he loved calling Elsie 'Cherie'. His eldest brother John who was also serving in Europe came on a visit one day to meet our family, a visit which I think was just to see what kind of people Bob was becoming involved with. We must have passed the inspection however, as shortly afterwards, although I doubt if it would have made any difference, Bob walked down the long back garden to where mother was busy taking some soft fruit off the bushes for a pie, and asked her for her permission to marry Elsie. Apparently mother gave her consent after adding, "So you really want to marry that feather-brained daughter of mine.", or words to that affect. Bob did, so he and Elsie became engaged.

One weekend when Elsie and I were out for a walk she tentatively produced a book from her bag and handed it to me saying that I should read it. When I opened it and looked at a couple of the pages I was both shocked and disgusted and felt quite sick. I hurriedly shut it again and handed it back to her, telling her that I didn't want to read it. It was a text book explaining the 'facts of life'. I had never dreamt that men and women behaved like that and that babies were produced that way., I was so shocked. I was about fifteen or sixteen at the time. I imagine that from the way Elsie acted and the clues she gave out, that she herself was, until she was about the same age, just as ignorant of these facts. Mother slipped up badly in this important education for her offspring. I think she just couldn't face the embarrassment involved, and in those days this subject was not included in the school's itinerary.

We were still spending our nights in the Anderson shelter as the air-raids continued to batter all over London. One morning upon leaving the shelter we were told by the Air-raid Wardens that there was an unexploded bomb in our front garden, and that the army were coming to dig it out and immobilize it, and we were to keep well out of the way. The army came and worked on the bomb and eventually managed to remove it safely for which of course we were most grateful. Mother however, was very annoyed with the men for digging up all her rose bushes and ruining her garden and told them all quite forcibly about it! She was more worried and upset about her plants than she was about the bomb. That was mother!

I was cycling home from work one evening during an air-raid when I heard a strange sound coming from an Aeroplane engine. Looking up as I went along a road beside a park I could see the 'plane' travelling across the sky, it was quite low and a short distance away on the other side of the park. As I watched I thought it was a small damaged plane going to crash. Then suddenly the strange sounding engine stopped and it plunged down and there was a terrible explosion. When I got home I told mother about it. The following day or two we discovered that it was Hitler's new weapon, a 'Doodle-bug', or 'Buzz Bomb', a type of flying explosive missile. These were terrible, and were used frequently. We used to hear the engines and pray that they wouldn't cut out above, or near us. They were diabolical weapons, and extremely nerve-racking. Sometime later Hitler introduced.yet another terrifying weapon, this time it was a powerful rocket which was unheard or unseen until it hit its target. Both of these weapons were far worse than the bombs, and caused havoc. We were told on the wireless that our aircraft and our Allies the Americans were doing all they could to find and destroy the actual sources of these new weapons, and would soon do so. So we continued to hope and pray. ...

Chapter 5

Early in June 1944 we heard the news from the wireless that ours and the American forces had successfully invaded Normandy, sustaining heavy losses. From the Cinema news films we saw some of the landings and the vicious fighting, woundings and killings that went on. While we were of course cheered by the news of the invasion and the courageous fighting of our forces, we were also heartbroken at the cost, and to this very day still are. It had to be, that is the tragedy. The Allies continued to fight their way successfully right across Europe and into Germany. It eventually ended with the defeated Germany's surrender in May,1945 following Hitler's suicide. The horrors discovered by the Allies which had been perpetrated by Hitler's Nazi Party during the war shocked the world, especially the terrible suffering and slaughter that had taken place in camps like Austwitch. The collapse of Germany and the end of the war in Europe brought great happiness, joy, and freedom everywhere and was celebrated all over the world with dancing, singing, street parties and wild abandon. Church bells rang out all over England. Bells that had remained silent for almost six years because we knew that they would only be rung as the warning of a German invasion. It was all so wonderful. No more air-raids, black outs, uncomfortable nights in the Anderson shelter, no more terrible Buzz bombs or Rockets to fear etc., The food and clothes ratiioning would continue for some time, but we were used to that, and it was not life threatening. The war would not be over we knew until of course Japan had been defeated, and now all efforts were concentrated in that direction.

On Saturday, August 4th 1945, a beautiful summer's day, Elsie and Bob were married at St.Elisabeth's church. (Strangely enough it was the same church where all those years previously I had been wrongly accused of stealing apples.)

It was a white wedding, with four bridesmaids consisting of Edith, Beryl Elsie's friend, myself, and Bella's daughter Eileen. I was once again, so terribly nervous that walking down the Aisle behind Elsie, I had an attack of the giggles. I don't think it was all that noticeable however, thank goodness. Elsie looked so very beautiful in her lovely white dress, and Bob so handsome, smart, and happy in his uniform. George gave Elsie away, also dressed splendidly in his Mercantile Marine uniform. The church was crowded with family members, and I think by the look of it, an invasion of all the Yanks in Bob's Company causing quite a furore amongst the neighbours!! Unfortunately because of the rationing situation, there was no sitdown reception, but everyone celebrated the wedding at the local public house. Bob's Company were destined to go to France so he was only allowed two days leave and had to be back at the base on Monday. Their dream of a honeymoon on the Isle of Wight had to be forgone to their dismay. Bob's Company did not go to France however, but within a few months returned to the U.S.A. Elsie had to remain at home awaiting the order and instructions to leave on a designated ship to join him.

The war with Japan continued until finally, in an attempt to end the bloody carnage, America dropped the first Atomic Bomb on Hiroshima which caused such desruction and devastation it horrified the world. Even then Japan refused to capitulate until a second one was dropped on Nagasaki. They finally surrendered on the 14th September,1945,(signed officially on 2nd September,1945.) The second World War was now over and VJ day was celebrated all over the world with great joy, here in the UK on the 15th September,1945. Peace at last, but at a terrible cost of loss of life and suffering. Everyone prayed most desperately that there would never be another war.

Gradually, demobilisation of our forces took place and men and women returned happily to civilian life. The members of my family with them, much to mother's great relief. George and his wife got back together again and found somewhere to live nearby. Bella's husband Jim was released from the Navy and together with their two children, who had now returned from evacuation, lived in a house in the next district. Fred came home from sea and out of the Merchant Navy, and settled down to work in a car factory. I continued to work in the office of the Chemical Company, learning everything I could about every task in the Department. My nice woman Department Head left her job and the Supervisor took over as a Section Head. I no longer took shorthand dictation but became a full time typist, typing everything from memo's, orders, tenders, invoices and so on, no longer the 'office girl'. I recall that in the winter we often had to wear our outdoor coats and even fingerless gloves to type we were so cold. The hearting system often failed.Men began to appear in the offices taking over the positions of Department Heads from the women who had performed the tasks satisfactorily throughout the war, and other more junior clerical jobs.

Fred, who had had a number of girl friends, one in New Zealand whom he had decided to marry a few years previously and then changed his mind, and a very nice girl called Mary in the next street, suddenly decided to marry another local girl instead. One called Lillian who was an ex Land Army Girl. Mother wasn't at all happy about the marriage, (as it is with most mothers, they never consider any girl to be worthy of their sons), and she refused to attend the wedding ceremony. He asked me to be a bridesmaid, but although I loved Fred very much, I was torn between loyalty to mother and his request. So I did not go to the wedding, neither did Elsie who was still at home waiting for the orders and a ship to take her to the U.S.A.to be with Bob. As far as I can remember, none of our family attended. I was told afterwards that it all went very well, and so the couple set up home together in London.

(Another chick had flown the nest).

No workmen appeared on the scene to dig out and remove the now unused Anderson Shelter, so I decided to tackle the job myself one weekend. I just couldn't wait to see the back of it! So wearing a pair of Elsie's old Land Army dungarees, which I often did when working in the garden, and using a spade, I shifted all the piled up earth on top of the shelter and eventually, after a long hard day's work managed to expose the bolted corrugated iron structure. (I was watched all the time by Bella's young son Ronnie who appeared to find the whole episode interesting, or perhaps even amusing.) To actually unbolt and remove this structure was of course beyond my capabilities so on one of their usual visits Bob and Teddy happily dealt with it. The only big problem now was to fill in the large hole that remained in the ground so that it could be used once again for growing vegetables. This I decided would take some time, so I thought the best thing to do was to fill it in gradually, which I did over the next couple of weeks. The neighbour next door was extremely impressed by my actions, and from then on referred to me as "a farmer's boy'. Mother was delighted to regain the ground for all her beloved gardening, and just couldn't wait to start planting.

Chapter 6.

In the Spring of 1946 Elsie was delivered of a beautiful baby girl in the front bedroom by mother. The two nurses were late in coming, and the doctor unavailable until the following day. The baby was named Jean after Bob's mother. During the Labour, hearing Elsie's cries and screams downstairs, I became so upset that I had to run down to the other end of the long garden to escape. I just couldn't bear to hear and know that she was suffering so much pain, I loved her so. (Although I cannot remember it at all I was told later that my half-brother George was in the living room and played the piano loudly to drown out Elsie's cries). When it was all over mother told me to go up and see Elsie and the new baby, and although washed out and tired Elsie was fine. I thought that I had never seen a prettier baby. I can remember almost boring my working colleagues to death talking about it. When Bob received the news he was delighted, and impatient to be reunited with Elsie and his new daughter. It was six weeks or more before Elsie got the word to board the ship that was taking the G.I. brides to America to join their husbands, even then when the authorities discovered how young the baby was they were a little apprehensive about accepting Elsie and Jean on the voyage. Mother was upset and I of course was heart broken when Elsie and the baby left England. I often think now how brave Elsie was to leave her home and family at the age of nineteen, and travel to take up residence in a strange country with a new husband, and the family that she had never met. Thank God she was one of the lucky ones, as many of the women who had married Americans found to their dismay that the places or homes were not quite what they had been told they were or what they had expected. Some arrived to find only wooden cabins or shacks to live in out in the wilds, or so forth. We heard fairly quickly from Elsie that all was well and that she had been made most welcome by Bob's family. There was some upset however, as Bob's mother was a dedicated Catholic although Bob was not interested very much in religion, and said that as they hadn't been married in a Catholic Church she believed that they were not really married and that made Jean illegitimate. They were then to please her re-married in a Catholic Church, and at the same time Elsie decided to change her religion. That was her choice and decision. The frequent letters we received from Elsie told us that they had settled down in Plymouth and were very happy, to our delight and relief.

Now there was only the two of us left, mother and myself at home and it felt very strange and the house so very quiet and empty. I missed Elsie very much as we were so close, and also Bob's pleasant weekend visits. The rest of the family, apart from Alec as he lived a fair distance away, visited us from time to time. Mother continued with her outdoor working routine and I carried on with my job in the offices of the Chemical Company.

At holiday times I took mother on all-day coach trips to the sea-side towns, and in 1948 I took her along with a friend and her mother who worked with my mother at the time, to the Isle of Wight for a week. We had a lovely time and really enjoyed ourselves. Mother nearly found herself with a man-friend in the boarding house, he was really taken with her but of course she wanted none of it . We all had a good laugh about it.

At that period of time we were all into letter writing and had
'pen=pals'. One of the girls in the office came to me one
day and asked if she could add my name and address to her
list of girls willing to write to a group of soldiers in an army
barracks. I agreed and after a few weeks received a letter from
Eric of the R.E.M.E. We became 'pen-pals' and exchanged
photographs and after a while he asked if he could visit me
on his next leave. After giving it a lot of thought I agreed and
mother said it would be O.K. for him to come to the house,
which he did one weekend. He wasn't terribly handsome but
had a nice face and a quiet well behaved manner. He was a
country boy and lived in Kelmscott in the Cotswold Hills
with his mother and father who ran the Plough Inn, a small
countryside public house.   He returned to his barracks and
we continued to correspond. When he got his next leave he
asked me if I would go with him to Kelmscott for a weekend
and meet his parents. He said he would drive me down there
in his father's car and bring me back afterwards. After giving
it a great deal of thought and with mother's agreement also,
I accepted. It was quite a long drive but the countryside was
fantastically beautiful and I thoroughly enjoyed it. He was
an excellent driver and said that when he left the army his
ambition was to start a taxi-service in the country. The Plough
Inn was a lovely little place, and his mother and father were
busy quiet country folk. I never went into the bar at all, but
imagine that it was quite small and know that it was not at
all noisy. Not like the town public houses. His mother settled
me in a very nice bedroom and made me welcome, but had
to keep disappearing to I believe help her husband.   The
following day Eric showed me around the village, then as he
was unfortunately, a football fan took me into Swindon in
the afternoon to watch a match. It was January, very cold and
frosty but dry and I was absolutely frozen and bored to tears
watching grown men run up and down a field chasing a ball.
I did not like football at all I discovered., and my opinion has

never altered. Eric was the first young man that I had ever gone out with and I was extremely shy and self-conscious, but he gave me the impression that I was his first girl friend too. That evening he drove me into Swindon once more but never said where he was taking me, said it was a surprise. We ended up at a large theatre where we thoroughly enjoyed watching a kind of music-hall performance, returning to the Plough Inn rather late that night. The weekend was extremely nice and enjoyable and I was driven home as promised on Sunday. That was my first experience of being entertained by a young man, which ended with my first quick gentle kiss. We continued to correspond and over a period of time he sent me a number of gifts one of which was a white silk scarf embroidered with his military badge and my name. It was lovely. I made several of these trips to Kelmscott with Eric on his army leaves, on one of which he invited mother and she loved it there too. Unfortunately he became serious about what I considered to be our friendship, and talked about marriage all the time. I told him quite often that I did not want to get married at all, even said quite firmly that I was going to be a 'career woman". The last letter I received from him was a marriage proposal saying that he had been offered a house in the village and was anxiously awaiting my answer, so please say " yes". My reply of course was a firm but gentle no. I liked Eric but the only thing I was sorry about was that it was such a beautiful place to live in - but definitely not to have to marry to live there!

There were two more baby girls born in our front bedroom with mother's and the doctor's aid. Not at the same time of course. They were both Edith's and Peter's offspring Sheila and Moira, sisters for Margaret. The couple were still living in the flat over the fish and chip shop at the time, but mother managed by certain methods to wangle them a two bed roomed council house a few streets away. They settled in there quite comfortably. Shortly afterwards because there was a narrow alleyway by the side of our house which during the war had sheltered Air Raid Wardens hiding for a crafty smoke and natter, and also many loving couples, and was now being used by louts and children to throw old rubbish and bicycles etc., over the fence into our back garden, mother became stressed and ill. She then asked the council for a transfer into another house. I was unhappy about this as I loved the house I had been raised in. So we moved into another two bed roomed house a short distance away. I never liked the new place at all. We had to share a gateway and path in the front and the back garden was very small, not at all like the one we had left.

Mother being almost desperate to move had accepted the first one she was offered. There was however, a bathroom upstairs in this house, without a wash-hand basin, but as the water pump provided on the iron copper downstairs never worked, we found that we had to carry the buckets of hot water up the flight of stairs every time we wanted a bath, and still had to have our daily washes in the kitchen sink. The house itself was always very cold and extremely difficult to heat. It was so cold one winter that the water tank in the loft froze and then later burst, and the bathroom taps had long icicles hanging from them. Two doors away there was a huge church and every Sunday its loud discordant bells would clang out for at least an hour attempting unsatisfactorily to play the tunes of Hymns. The noise of them was deafening. I love religious music and all the well known Hymns, but.......I could no longer ride my bicycle to work and had to take the underground train, but not too far, just two stations away. Mother had to give up her school cleaning job, but I was pleased about that as I knew that it was to much for her now. Instead she took on flat cleaning for a teacher a short distance away and still continued to take in sewing on her old treddle sewing machine. Her thin old legs would peddle away there for hours on end. It worried me and I vowed that if she wanted to carry on sewing

I would manage to buy her an Electric sewing machine one day, and I did. The working of it puzzled her at first but she soon got used to it and loved it, and it made me feel a little easier in my mind, although I would have preferred her to rest more and stop taking in so much sewing. Hopefully, none at all! She was determined to carry on though and I hated her latest and as I thought really trying venture. That of turning Ex Government Women's Land Army britches into shorts for men, for the Army and Navy Stores. Large bundles of these were frequently, too frequently I considered, brought into the house for her and all she received for this task was nine pence for each pair of shorts. Disgusting payment I thought for the work involved. I had of course no say in the matter. Bundles of these britches just kept arriving keeping mother hard at work, and littering up the living room. (On my way home from the office every week I used to buy mother a bottle of tonic wine namely "Wincarnis" or "Sonatagin", or sometimes if neither of these were available, a bottle of Guinness. Hoping that it would help to keep her fit and well.)

Chapter 7.

Quite often on a Sunday I would take a bus into Bermondsey, London to visit Fred and Lilian in their flat. It wasn't a very nice district and they badly wanted to find a house in Dagenham. After some time their wish was granted and the council allocated them a Pre-fabricated house on a new estate within the Dagenham area. These were lovely houses, some constructed on the bungalow style, others two storied. They had been manufactured and introduced during the war as temporary relief for the housing shortage, and only intended for usage for up to ten years maximum. They were however, so well built that they remained in use for a great many years afterwards. George and Marion were allocated one, also Bella and Jim, and they were all well pleased. I liked these houses very much, they were a lot better than the ordinary brick built ones both in comfort, design and appearance.

At work my spitefully natured Section Head at last decided that she had had enough of the job and retired, to everyone's delight. As I, although the youngest member of the department, now had a complete knowledge of all the working functions carried out, I was promoted to Section Head in her place. I was quite proud and pleased, although I kew it was going to be a difficult task controlling older, mostly married staff. And it was! The new male Department Head also hadn't a clue about the running of, and the intricacies of, dealing with the documentation processes involved , and relied on me to guide him through them.   With this promotion I had been hoping or rather, expecting a large salary increase, but was disappointed with the amount given.   I had been told that Chemical Companies were quite poor wage payers, now I had personal knowledge of the truth of this information.   I stayed on there however, always hoping for a change in the Company's policy, and also because I had no desire to join the huge Commuting throng to London for employment.   I was also promoted to what the Company termed "Senior Staff", put onto a monthly salary instead of a weekly one, and given four weeks holiday instead of two. (During our working hours I recall that a Mobile X-ray Van was regularly set up outside the building and everyone, department by department, had to go and have a chest X-ray for Tuberculosis, which disease in time was wiped completely out of Britain.)

My half-brother Alec had by then given up his bungalow and job in March, Cambs., because his wife had started to suffer with chest and breathing problems due to the dampness of the Fenlands, and now lived in a town nearby. His daughter Pearl had just left school and he asked me to try to get her a job in my Chemical Company so I contacted the Personnel Dept., gave her a good reference and they gave her a job in the Filing Pool, which was the only vacancy they had at the time. She appeared to be quite happy and settled there.

One day I discovered that the girl in the office who had sent my name and address to the army barracks for a pen-pal some months previously, had now sent it to the sailing crew on the Frigate HMS.Superb. I therefore received a letter from a sailor called Fred.   We corresponded and forwarded photographs as usual. He came from Durham in the North of England and we became good friends. I called him Laurie because I preferred it to Fred and he didn't mind at all. With mother's permission he visited the house whenever he obtained leave and took me out to the cinema's and so forth, and we got on well together. One thing I did find quite embarrassing was upon leaving the cinemas in full view of everyone, he always needed me to put my arms around him and hold down his sailor's collar so that he could put on his overcoat, I was still that shy. Mother appeared to like him quite a lot, as of course she had Eric. In the summer as I have always been keen on boats and ships I suggested to Laurie, mother, and my half sister Bella who was staying with us at the time, that it might be a good idea to spend a week's holiday on the Norfolk Broads. They all agreed quite happily although not one of us knew the first thing about sailing a yacht. We rented a four berth yacht for a week and upon our arrival in Norfolk were shown to it's berth and without a word of instruction or advice, taken out into midstream on it and deserted by the man in charge, who quickly disappeared over the side into a dingy and rowed away. We were all rather startled by this and of course didn't know quite what to do next. There we were sailing merrily along through all kinds of other vessels without a clue apart from guiding it with the tiller, which we all instinctively and cowardly left in the hands of Laurie. He was the trained sailor after all, - but unfortunately not with yachts! As you can imagine it was quite an exciting week, but alas a terrifying one for Bella who wished from the start that she hadn't come along. She crouched down in the well of the boat half inside the cabin entrance, and continually cried out for us to stop, even if it meant tying up to a blade of bankside grass! There were no brakes of course and the only way we finally managed to stop was when we hit a mud bank, then quickly hauled down the sails. Alas it had no engine or outboard motor to propel it just a jib and mainsail. Mother was fine and appeared to enjoy herself and Laurie and I learned quite a bit about sailing that week, but didn't repeat the experience. As usual I kept the friendship between Laurie and myself strictly platonic and sadly after a while we lost touch with each other. Bella, (short for Isabella Ella Barr, named after mother) never wanted to repeat the yachting holiday, I think she'd had enough. (Bella, like Alec had brown hair but otherwise was quite domineering in her manner, not a bit quiet. She was also quite shrewd, and had a good sense of humour. She was quite nevous when being driven by her husband in their car, a nagging backseat driver! At one time she and her husband Jim ran a large public house for a while. Otherwise she was a machinist in a factory.)

Mother and I became quite close companions and she would meet me from work near a cinema once a week and we would then keep abreast of all the good films. Sometimes one of my office friends would come along with us. I would also go on long cycle rides with Fred, or when he got a motor cycle I would ride on the pillion all the way to Southend approximately twenty miles away, especially at night to see the famous lights there. His wife Lilian never seemed to mind these excursions, as she spent the time visiting her own family nearby. Holiday times I would take mother away to the coast for a week or two and we both enjoyed it. After a while my half-brother George, whose wife had taken a job in a factory and spent all her evenings playing Bingo, had his dinner after work with mother and I twice a week, and joined us on our holiday jaunts. The man living next door to us gave me an address of friends of his in Guernsey, the Channel Islands and I wrote to them and asked if they could put mother and I up for two weeks holiday in the coming summer. They quickly replied that they would be pleased to have us. We caught the appropriate ferry and had a glorious fortnight with them, visiting all the islands around. I did not like the island of Jersey very much and preferred Guernsey. Jack and Ethel were extremely nice Chapel people and showed us around all the fortifications built by the Germans during their occupation in the war, and told us of their experiences with the invaders whilst they were there, as well as taking us around all the beauty spots. They had suffered quite a lot one way and another, and it was very interesting. They even had to take a young German soldier into their home as a lodger during the occupation. We all got on very well together and became firm friends and from then on they visited us for holidays and vice versa for many years, even after Ethel had died.

At first, after Ethel passed away and because Jack and I had become so close, he expressed the wish that I would marry him and live in Guernsey. I was still however, uninterested in the marital state, and so we remained good friends and continued with the holiday arrangements even after he met and married his new wife Alice, who was pleased to accompany him on the visits.

Years later George, who like me, was also interested in boats, took me along to Leigh-on-Sea and we looked at a second hand boat called "The Windward" which was for sale. It was a 30 ft., old type sailing barge which also possessed an engine. It needed some attention, especially in the engine department, and the owner wanted to sell it for £150. George and I spent two or three hours examining the boat and discussing the price before he decided to purchase it. From then on the two of us spent every weekend at Leigh-on-Sea working on the boat. The only problem was that when the tide was out to reach it we had to wade knee deep through thick black mud which was rather off-putting. However we persevered. We did a lot of work on the boat and George finally got the engine running so mother and I spent a holiday week 'roughing it' with him on it. We didn't get very far out though before the wretched engine gave out again. We managed to get back to our mooring place and took mother back home, before starting working hard on the boat again the following weekend. This procedure went on for many months both winter and summer. However, after sand -papering and re-varnishing the huge sixty foot mast innumerable times, and carrying out many other tasks, I gave up. I'm afraid George was never quite satisfied. He was a perfectionist being a Master Carpenter, and carried on the work by himself, finally almost taking the "Windward" to pieces and re-building it from scratch! George was a quiet person, never complained about shoddy workmanship to me and was grateful for any help. He was dark haired, and very handsome with a great sense of humour and devilment. He was still working on the boat during weekends when sadly he became ill with heart trouble, eventually dying suddenly of a heart attack at the age of sixty four, one year before retiring. It was such a shock and great tragedy, and broke mother's heart. She never quite got over his death. Needless to say I was also very upset, as were the rest of the family. Mother and I used to go frequently to visit, take flowers, and tidy his grave after the funeral although the Cemetery was a fair distance away.

Elsie corresponded with us often and after saving quite hard, mother and I offered and arranged a trip for her, to come back home on the liner "Batory" for a three month visit. She now had three small children whom she brought with her while Bob stayed in America working. It was so wonderful to see Elsie again and have her back home with us. Unfortunately she was a bad sailor and hadn't enjoyed the trip at all, suffering greatly from sea-sickness. She was however, very happy to see us and visit all the rest of the family and some of her old friends. I was still working but we had the evenings and weekends to spend together and it was quite like old times. Elsie told us all about her new life in Plymouth, Massachusettes, Bob's family, and the friends she had made there and that she was very happy, but of course that naturally she missed the family. The three little ones she brought with her were Jean, Michael, and the baby was Philip, they were adorable, but quite a handful,

I wondered how ever she had managed on the ship being so ill with sea-sickness as well. It must have been very difficult for her. (I recall that the year she came over was the year that I officially 'came of age' at twenty-one, when I could be given the 'key of the door'. I had of course already had it for a good many years!) We were all once again, when the time came for her return to America, very upset to say goodbye and missed her terribly.

I was still very interested in writing and spent some of my spare time scribbling away. One day I discovered that a young man living only across the road from me called Harold, was also very interested in becoming a Writer. We spent some time chatting and decided to start a Young Writer's Club as he knew a few others who were also dabbling with the idea. There were about six of us, all still young, and we began to meet in Harold's house every week to compare notes. During one of these meetings we decided to start our own magazine called "The Young Writer", and I was nominated the editor. Why they chose me I don't know as I haven't a clue about editing. We enjoyed our sessions together and turned out between us, we thought, a good typewritten edition. I considered the contents weren't bad for amateurs and said so in the editorial. Unfortunately, when the local paper obtained a copy the editor was not quite so complementary and said so. We therefore refrained from writing further editions! After a while, sad to say, our club meetings gradually came to an end.

Chapter 8

I was, and still am, extremely fond of animals. Mother also cared for them, so when a friend showed me a beautiful Welsh Collie that he had bought, I eagerly asked mother's permission to buy one myself. She agreed so I sent away to Wales, he had given me the address, and bought a wonderful Collie dog. It arrived by goods train at my local station where I collected it. He was really lovely, and was like the film dog Lassie except that he was black and white, with a tinge of brown on the cheek bones. I fell in love with him at once, so did mother when I took him home. I called him Laddie, not very original I know. He was only six months old but quite big, quiet and rather nervous. I think the train journey was a bit too nerve racking for him. He soon settled down however, and was quick to learn the house rules etc., and was great company. We spent a great deal of time at the weekends and in the evenings roaming the local parks and streets together, enjoying every minute. Being a thoroughbred though he unfortunately picked up quite a few health problems quite easily, starting with a bad case of Distemper. The Vet., told me to keep him warm and gave me some medication for him. Mother was as concerned as I was, and one evening when I returned home from work I was greeted at the front door by a somewhat startling gambolling apparition. It turned out to be Laddie, who mother, to keep him warm, had found an old green flannel jacket and dressed him up in it. He looked ridiculous, but warm! His two front legs were encompassed in the jacket sleeves, and the jacket buttons were done up securely underneath. Trust mother to think of something like that. I couldn't stop laughing at the sight of him. It must have done the trick, as he soon recovered his health, but I'll never forget it. Later on in his life Laddie suffered from Arthritis in his hind legs and Fred, putting him in the side-car, and with me riding on the pillion, used to run him by motorbike to the Vet., in Romford every week for Gold Injections. I was extremely grateful for Fred's help with this problem. I don't know what I'd have done without it as I could not have afforded a taxi at that time. The Vet., fees were expensive enough. I really loved that dog. Sometime later someone presented mother with a beautiful blue budgerigar which we both grew very fond of, and spent a great deal of time and attention teaching it to talk. Laddie became extremely jealous because of the fuss we made of the budgie and would push his way to the front, to let us know that he was still there. He never attempted to harm the bird at all, simply resented the attention we gave it. Just like an only child resents the sudden appearance of a baby brother or sister in the family.

Several months later after saving as much as possible I managed to buy mother a Burco Twin Tub washing machine, deciding that if the washing was done at the weekends, I could help out, or even do the lot myself. Mother was of course delighted, but would definitely not have any washing at all done on a Sunday. It was the Sabbath! She really put her foot down about this, and once because I didn't abide with her decision, disappeared from the house for the whole of the day without a word to say where she was going. I was almost frantic with worry, but it wasn't until quite late in the evening when I was out in a nearby field taking Laddie for his walk, still worried sick, that she suddenly appeared and walked along with us. Mother refused to say where she had spent the whole day and was still very uptight and annoyed. It came out a few days later that she had taken the bus to Hainault forest and stayed there by herself just wandering about. From then on of course the washing was done between us on a Saturday morning before going out for the weekly shopping, and after some of the house- hold chores were dealt with.

In the evenings when sitting together mother used to tell me about events in her life. I was very interested in all she had to say. She had been told by her parents when she was quite small that her father, who was a hunchback, was the illegitimate son of the Duchess of Fife, which was why he was quite frequently visited by men in black frock coats and tall black hats. Her father also told her that he had curvature of the spine because as a child he had been put into an Institution, and strapped tightly to a wooden boarded bed for most of the day and night.

He had however, upon reaching a suitable age, been sent to college and became a Dental Surgeon. Mother had one brother, and three sisters, James, Wilhelmina, Elsie, and Annie who had died when quite young. Mother never told me the cause of her death, but she talked of the way she had stroked Annie's hair and tidied it as she lay dying, and how sad she felt. (Mother did say that when their parents died James made sure to take all the money they left for himself and had set himself up in a large Public House.) When mother was twelve years old she said, her mother sent her into Service as a Scullery Maid, and after several weeks she was so miserable and unhappy there, her hands were really painful, raw, and bleeding with chaps, that she ran all the way home again. Her mother simply scolded her severely and sent her back immediately to continue with the job that she had been given.

As far as I can gather it was whilst still in Service when she'd grown older, that she met and married her first husband called John, who was employed there as a Groom. Mother told me that they settled down in London, Hoxton I believe. They had four children, the first born, named John after his father, died at about three years of age from Pneumonia. During the First World War her husband, serving in the Army as a Rifle Man, was killed in France. Now a widow, mother took on many different kinds of jobs including some nursing in a hospital. She told me about the bombing by the Zeppelins in London. How she and the children had to shelter on the lower floor of a building called Underwood's below the stables of horses who, because of the noise of the bombing, panicked and kept stamping on the floor above them, frightening them more lest the trampling horses brought the ceiling crashing down on them.Apparently later, on a visit to her sister in Wales, mother discovered a small empty shop with suitable living accommodation, which was going for the same amount of rent, as the house she and her children were living in in London. She thereupon decided to move and take on the shop. Mother said that the shop was completely bare inside, no fittings at all, so she set to work and all by herself built the counters and shelves etc., simply out of used empty tea chests. She then started off her small business by cooking and providing luncheon snacks for customers, many of them school children. The shop did well and made a substantial profit, which in time greatly improved making mother very happy, even though she still had to work very hard to keep it going, and care for the children. The war was still going on and one day mother had a visit from a soldier who claimed to be a friend of her dead husband. His name was Thomas and he was home on leave from France. They got to know each other quite well and before he returned to France, after a subsequent leave, mother told me that he proposed to her. She admitted that she had only accepted him because she was so sure that, like her husband John, he would never survive the war. He did however, and "regrettably" they were married. It wasn't very long mother said before all the money she'd earned from the shop had disappeared in drink and gambling, and they returned to London. As mentioned in the first chapter Thomas turned out to be a womaniser, wife beater and alcoholic, and eventually died in an Asylum leaving mother with another four children.

Chapter 9

I had not yet managed to afford to buy a Television Set so when Elizabeth 11 was crowned in l953, mother and I went around to Edith and Peter's to watch the Coronation. Later on I rented a Black & White one from a shop in Barking and paid monthly for it. They dealt with any repairs incurred which was most convenient. Mother loved to watch the programmes of an evening, so did I. It was wonderful to see everything in the comfort of your own living room instead of always having to travel to a cinema. Not that we stopped our weekly cinema visits to see all the current films, they couldn't be missed if at all possible, and the price of the seats were not as expensive as they are nowadays. You could get a good seat in those days for only one shilling and nine pence!

I still worked in the Chemical Company as a Section Head in the Export Department, and in 1954, thinking how wonderful it would be to visit Elsie and Bob in America, I popped into the Company's Shipping Department simply to enquire about fares etc.,I was therefore utterly amazed when several days later the manager rang me in my office to say that mother and I were booked in a cabin on the Holland and America Liner ss" Maasdam", and on it's sister ship the ss" Ryndam" returning to Southampton three month's later! I had not yet even asked my boss for three month's leave of absence, and wasn't at all sure that when I did, it would be granted. I returned home from work that evening in some kind of daze. Fortunately mother, although very surprised at the prospect , was eager to go. Now, all I had to do was to see my boss, explain and obtain his permission. I did this the following morning when I entered his office. He was quite surprised but after giving my request some thought he granted it with the proviso that beforehand, I write down every documental procedure clearly in a notebook for them to use. This I did although it took some time, and I sorely regretted doing it some months later. Mother and I then of course went through the usual drill of obtaining passports etc., We had to go to the American Embassy in London and queue up to obtain a Visa. There after filling in forms we even had our finger prints taken, and were asked several times if we had someone in America to provide for us if necessary. That wasn't the exact wording, but that was the meaning, as if not the Visa's would not be granted. At that time Britain only allowed each person to take the sum of fifty pounds sterling out of the country. We also had to be vaccinated for Smallpox. (I had always wanted to travel and see the world, even especially to go to Switzerland and ski, and so I was very excited at the prospect.)

I went with mother to our doctor's surgery and we were given our Smallpox vaccinations, and told to return in a week's time to see if they had taken. When we did return we found two doctors there. Apparently our one was leaving, for which his patients were pleased as apparently he was often the worse for drink, and Dr. Dean was taking over. My vaccination had taken very well I was told, but mother's had turned Septic and required more treatment. Dr. Dean who was extremely nice and a very good doctor soon put the matter right. He was very interested in both of us and our trip.

A few days later I received baggage labels and instructions

regarding the voyage from the Holland & America Shipping Line. The sailing date was June 3rd.It was all very exciting, neither of us ever having travelled further than the Channel Islands. I admit to being slightly nervous of the journey, but had always loved ships and boats, and if I had been a man would have liked to have been be a sailor. (It didn't help my nerves at all having listened to a dramatic radio play broadcast the night earlier, called "The Kraken Wakes" which was about the rising of a terrible monster from the deep. Also having recently seen the film the "Titanic").

Fred, who now had three children, a son and two daughters, was kind enough to offer to take care of Laddie whilst we were away. I was very pleased about this as I really hated the thought of having to put him into kennels. I knew that he would now be well looked after. We also managed to pay three month's rent in advance for the house before we sailed, so that there wouldn't be any trouble about that. The sailing day came and we left for Southampton on the designated boat train. When we arrived we were taken on board a tender out to the ss."Maasdam" which was lying out off the Isle of Wight. It was a beautiful ship and we were welcomed aboard by a great many white coated stewards, one of which took us to our lovely cabin and made sure that we were comfortable. We felt like Royalty, we were treated so well. The steward introduced himself, told us about the necessary mealtimes etc., and I requested that he wakened us each morning at 7.30 am., with a cup of tea. (Just like 'Lady Muck'!) He did just as I asked every morning for the entire voyage, which lasted six days and nights and was fantastic. Mother said that being on the ship both going and returning, was the best holiday that she had ever had or wanted. I thought so too. At the start of the voyage we were shown our life-boat stations and instructed how to don our life-jackets which were in our cabin. Mealtimes were announced by a boy going around the ship with a delightfully toned miniature xylophone, and each meal consisted of seven courses which were delicious. Then we were given, or offered pieces of fruit to take away. The dining room was large and the tables beautifully laid out. Our dining steward was particularly nice, especially to mother, who he tried hard to encourage to have seconds of everything. All the crew of the ship were of Dutch origin, and spoke slightly broken but understandable English. The passengers appeared to be mostly American and were very friendly. There was no 'snobby' dressing up for meals, everyone dressed quite casually, which was extremely pleasant. We were very pleased about that. There was one instance on the final night of the trip over however, that one male passenger arrived for dinner in evening dress much to everyone's amusement, and a great deal of laughter and applause. Apparently his friend had told him that it was necessary, simply as a joke. The American passengers were always up to some kind of devilment for amusement, even to putting notices up on the board, one announcing' mutiny' and trying to talk the crew into causing a mutiny, later it was discovered that all the crew of the ship had held a meeting about the notice and it was hurriedly removed. Also a strike of 'long shore' men in New York and that the ship would go on to Halifax and then we would have to travel to NY by train. Others, the birth of a baby during the night, that the entire British Navy had passed us during the night, and so on. All of which caused slight confusion and consternation amongst the crew we were told. On board there was every kind of entertainment you could wish for from cinema films, dancing, classical concerts, theatre concerts and shows, bars, libraries, gymnastics, etc., and of course a swimming pool on deck. Mother and I spent most of our time on the deck in the wonderful fresh air watching the waves and so on, even when it was quite rough and there were life-lines everywhere, and everyone else stayed below, we loved it. As the ship sailed just off Newfoundland it became very foggy and the ship's horn was sounded repeatedly all night and day, so exciting! We were the only people on deck at these times, and believe it or not, never caught a glimpse of an Iceberg! Happily neither of us suffered the slightest bit of sea sickness, in fact we both enjoyed the swaying and rolling of the ship, I slept better there at night than I have ever slept, and that coming from a perpetual insomniac since the troubled nights experienced during the war, was really something. When we came into view of New York harbour and saw through a slight heat haze the Statue of Liberty, and all the small boats and ferries, it was so exciting.

The ship was first boarded by U.S. officials checking everyone's passports and papers etc., who, when completely satisfied, descended over the side of the ship back into the tender that had brought them alongside. The s.s."Maasdam" then proceeded to anchor at the dock side where a great number of people awaited it's arrival, including Elsie and Bob, all waving excitedly at the passengers including mother and I, arranged eagerly at the ship's rail returning their waves. Just like something you see in a movie. After descending the gangway we all queued up to be given our luggage taken from the ship's hold and laid out along the dockside. A kindly American Cop., who was in charge, walked along the queue and seeing mother, decided that as an elderly lady she should be moved with me to the front of the queue, and took us there. No one complained about this but unfortunately, because the Shipping Company had mistakenly sent me the incorrect luggage labels, we were the last to leave, everyone else having already gone, when after a great deal of difficulty I found ours. Elsie and Bob, now alone on the dock, still waited patiently for us to join them. When we did, and after a lot of hugging and greetings, we went to Bob's car and he took us to the Empire State Hotel which was situated at the gateway to Broadway and Manhattan, where he had booked us in for several nights to enable us to see something of New York before heading for Plymouth. So after resting and catching up on all the family news we had a wonderful time visiting all the famous places, and seeing all the sights.

Chapter 10

When we eventually left New York and drove into Plymouth we found that it was a fairly small, delightfully quiet sea-side town. I hadn't imagined it to be so lovely from Elsie's letters, although she had said how nice it was. While we were there I completely fell in love with it, and desperately wanted to stay.

Bob's family invited all their friends and gave us a ' welcome to America' party at a nearby hall, when we had settled in, which we thoroughly enjoyed. Elsie, Bob, and their now four young children shared a large detached house a little way from the town with one of his friends. The house was built into two completely separate apartments, Elsie and Bob lived on the first floor, and his friend Buster and family lived on the ground floor. Buster's wife Sheila was also an English 'war bride.'

Bob returned to work at his job in the local Cotton Mill while Elsie and the children showed us around the historical town of Plymouth. We visited the large Stone Portico over Plymouth Rock on which the Pilgrims from England had landed many years ago, the huge statue of Massassoit the Indian Chief who had given them so much help, and of course the replicas of the ship the "Mayflower", and the Pilgrim's village. I absolutely loved the picturesque white wooden churches with their tall spires and the Colonial style houses. There were quite a number of shops and restaurants along the front, the shops selling a lot of souvenirs for the tourists. (Whilst we were over there Elsie had a 'brainwave' one day and we both went into a shop and bought identical 'Matador' suits which at that time were the new 'thing'. We looked great!!) Opposite the wide sandy beach were three or four tennis courts in which Bob and I enjoyed playing. (Elsie couldn't play but couldn't resist having her photograph taken holding a racquet like a champion!) There was no charge for using these courts, unlike England, and there was a ruling that the juniors must leave them free for the seniors to use in the evenings. Mother, Elsie and I spent many afternoons on the beach with the children. Michael who was about six or seven years old used to spend a lot of time attacking the large Horseshoe Crabs that were crawling around, with small rocks trying to smash their hard shells. (When he was twenty-one years old sadly, Michael, serving as a Marine, was killed in the Vietnam war.)

Bob's hours in the cotton mill were two till ten, so to earn extra money he used to spend the mornings working for a lady called Mrs. Collins. She had a beautiful Colonial Style house a little way away and he was painting it for her and tending the grounds. He asked me if I would like to go with him and also earn a little, and help. I jumped at the chance. We left at eight every morning in his car and were back in time for lunch and his regular job. The house was lovely, set up on a cliff in plenty of lawn covered grounds. There was also a modern Bungalow in the grounds which Mrs. Collins used for herself and friends at weekends. The wage she paid was a dollar an hour and I thoroughly enjoyed helping Bob with the painting, and mowing all the grass etc., Mrs. Collins and some of her friends were there one weekend when we arrived, they were all sitting in garden recliners outside the bungalow. Bob introduced me to her and she made quite a fuss of me and insisted on me sitting with them and drinking a "Tom Collins". They were all extremely friendly.

I also spent some time with Bob and his friends 'target shooting' with his revolver. The targets were only empty bottles lined up on a fence, (I could never have shot anything living) and I really enjoyed it. I discovered that I wasn't such a bad shot. Guido, an Italian yank, and I got on well together and became good friends. He lived with his wife and young family nearby and often visited Elsie and Bob. We also met and made friends with George Holman and his mother Marie. George was a bachelor but inclined to drink quite a lot. He gave me a tiny calf called Pete and also a small heifer he had named Bobby. Of course he had to keep them housed in his barn and feed them, but assured me that they were mine. His mother Marie, a widow, was very friendly and came Blue-berry picking with us and became very close to mother, sending both mother and I quite expensive gifts when we returned to England, and writing us many newsy letters. George also decided to take us all horse riding one day and it was quite an occasion. Never having been on a horse before I was a bit shaken at the distance of the ground beneath me, it was a giant of a horse and I was glad to get back down on terra firma. Elsie's horse was a lot smaller than mine, and I was a bit put out about that! (Of course mother stayed with the children. - Not silly.) When I was back home in England Elsie wrote and told me that George had waylaid her one day and told her that when we returned to the States he was going to marry me and take me out hunting with him!! Nice!

Mother started to complain about pain in one of her shoulders one day which after a few more days apparently became a lot worse, so Elsie arranged an appointment for her with her own doctor. We took her along and after an examination she was given an X-ray which showed that she was suffering with a Frozen Shoulder. The doctor gave her a prescription and advice about gentle exercise for the shoulder and charged me $10. We obtained the pills on the prescription from the local Pharmacy and I had to pay $14. That was all the money I had earned from Mrs. Collins so far. I was very glad that I had it. Poor mother suffered quite a lot with that shoulder but gradually by constantly exercising it the problem disappeared. I discovered then that the question of health practise in America could be very expensive if you lived there. Everyone had to have some kind of health insurance for the costs involved.

The surrounding countryside was beautiful, it was scattered with large lakes (which they happily called ponds), and tall majestic trees almost reaching up to the skies. We bathed in the lakes, had wonderful picnics on the luscious grass and the weather was lovely, not once did it rain all the time we were there. Bob also took us all in the car to a Drive-in-Movie which in itself was quite an experience. In fact we did and tried everything. I even worked for a day in a local small printers where certain newspapers and advertising articles were dealt with. The huge guillotine was a little nerve racking and I made sure to avoid using that. The owner of the place was elderly and very nice to be with. Elsie wrote to me later in England and told me that he had accidentally cut his thumb off with the guillotine, so perhaps I was wise not to try to use it. When we visited the government office for Income Tax before coming home as specified, the gentleman who welcomed us in and dealt with our papers was certain that there were very many places that would quite happily give me employment, and practically offered me a Job there, which made me all the more determined to return to the States as soon as possible. I really didn't want to leave. I loved the people and their casual life style and was convinced that both mother and I would be happy there. Elsie and Bob also appeared keen on the idea and began to suggest various housing plans for us to consider. Cheaper types of Mobile Homes Elsie said were ideal and were well built and in ideal surroundings and would probably suit for a start. I was all for it. Mother appeared more cautious, although she agreed that we could return for good the following year. Elsie and the children were very excited about the idea and of course the children were anxious to have Laddie to look after as I had told them all about him and showed them snapshots of him.

On the day of our departure Bob drove us to New York with Elsie and we said our very tearful goodbyes before boarding the "Ryndam". We stood at the ship's rail very unhappily, (or at least I was),with the other passengers and waved our farewells as Elsie stood with Bob's arm around her, sobbing her heart out. I was heartbroken and hated the thought of returning to my old way of life, not so much as not wishing to see my beloved England.

The routine and lay-out of the" Ryndam" was identical to her sister ship the "Masdam" and once again the crew were mainly of Dutch origin and the majority of the passengers American. I must confess that I was not at all a suitable companion for mother or anyone at that time as I was so consumed with misery and unhappiness. I perked up a little after a couple of days feeling very guilty about my behaviour, and joined mother on deck in the fresh air and various activities. One of the Dutch stewards appeared to take a particular interest in me and spent a great deal of his time trying to win me over. His name was Joe (he pronounced it 'Yoh'), I accepted and enjoyed his various attentions such as bringing me small gifts of fresh fruit and trays of afternoon tea etc., to the cabin, but was wise enough not to take any of it seriously, knowing or having read, all about the antics of ship stewards on their many voyages. After all my brother was a ship's steward at one time. We had some rough weather but on the whole the trip home went quite smoothly, finishing in Southampton docks from where we took the boat train to Waterloo and then the underground to our local station.

Chapter 11

We were home. Back to our wonderful surroundings of row after row of identical council houses and busy tarmac roads. No beautiful open country scenery, lakes or tall trees. No wonder I felt quite miserable. Not mother though who appeared to be happy to be back in our small house once again and quite settled even though she said with great conviction that it was the best holiday that she had ever had.   I was of course delighted to welcome Laddie back when Fred brought him, and he made such a great fuss of us.   Fred and his family had taken good care of him as I knew they would. He was extremely fit and well and glad to be with us again. (Laddie lived for a full thirteen and a half years until he had a severe stroke and had to be put down. I was heart broken.)

When I returned to my Office job in the Chemical Company, I must confess rather unenthusiastically, I discovered with surprise and a great deal of shock that my boss had given my position as Section Head to his girlfriend, with of course the use of my book of written instructions!! There was simply nothing for me to do but sit at an empty desk, much to my previous staff's amusement.   He could not however fire me which was something anyway. I could, and should have, gone to the Personnel Department and registered my complaint, but I neglected to do so and quietly accepted the new arrangement. I began to learn the other part of the large department's work which dealt with exports to the Far East. Also, in the meantime, while there was nothing else to occupy me, I spent the working day amusing myself by writing a great deal of verse etc., quite enjoying myself doing so, and also knowing that I was still regularly being paid by the Company. (Within a very short period of time my verse became quite popular with the rest of the staff and I received a large number of requests for specified events and occasions, which I happily fulfilled.)

I was soon given a Senior executive position in this part of the department and dealt with pricing and sending out written quotations , government tenders, and telephone quotations including delivery dates and so forth to numerous customers. The only real difficulty with these, mainly the telephone enquiries was that I, unfortunately did not possess a chemist's knowledge and many of the names etc., were completely confusing. I had been given a thick booklet of chemical synonyms and had to spend considerable time wading through looking for the various names of the chemicals required. The customers always appeared to request quotations for products with different names, especially when on the telephone. It was quite frustrating, but I got there eventually. (I wrote a long verse about this in my spare time). We now covered Fine Chemicals, Plastics, Photographic products, Agricultural, and Laboratory chemicals as well. Quite a selection!

I still wanted desperately to return to the States and was waiting for mother to name the day and the time. Every time I mentioned it she said "we'll go next year". So I waited. And waited. The years were rolling by. Elsie and Bob also waited expectantly. It eventually became quite apparent that mother no longer wished to go. I think that she did not want to leave with the prospect of perhaps never seeing the rest of the family again, I don't know, she never said.

What could I do? I couldn't leave her on her own. I would never have been at peace with myself, I loved her so very much. Depression began to set in… I had so longed for a change of scene and possibly of employment, and the prospect of being closer to Elsie and Bob. It was hard to accept and bear.I tried hard to settle down and conquer my great disappointment but my depression grew and grew.

I eventually made an appointment with Dr. Dean. He had been extremely efficient and kind with my previous ailments, even to refusing to accept the customary money for certificates and when possible providing me with a card for lower cost prescriptions. He was always, mother said dropping into our house to spend several minutes talking to her and resting, then filling in his various forms whilst he was there. Mother was so very sure as she always told me that he had a very soft spot for me, in fact she was convinced that he 'was in love with me', of all things. Anyway, he was as I said very helpful so I decided to confide in him. He listened, and when I told him that I was very often in tears for no apparent reason and could no longer find any pleasure in life etc., he arranged for me to have Out-Patient treatment at a local Psychiatric Hospital, which I did, having the customary ECT treatment, but sadly it proved unsatisfactory and no help whatsoever. My depression simply got worse and worse as time went by and in the end I no longer wanted to go on living, it got that bad!Unbelievable, but true.I decided that something had to be done so regrettably in the nineteen sixty's went into the Psychiatric Hospital as a voluntary patient.

Elsie & Phyllis. 1954

Edith, Mother, George, Elsie, Alec, & Fred. 1968

Elsie, Alec, & Bella. 1982

Elsie, mother, & Phyllis. 1954

Mother's parents, & siblings

Mother & Phyllis. 1954

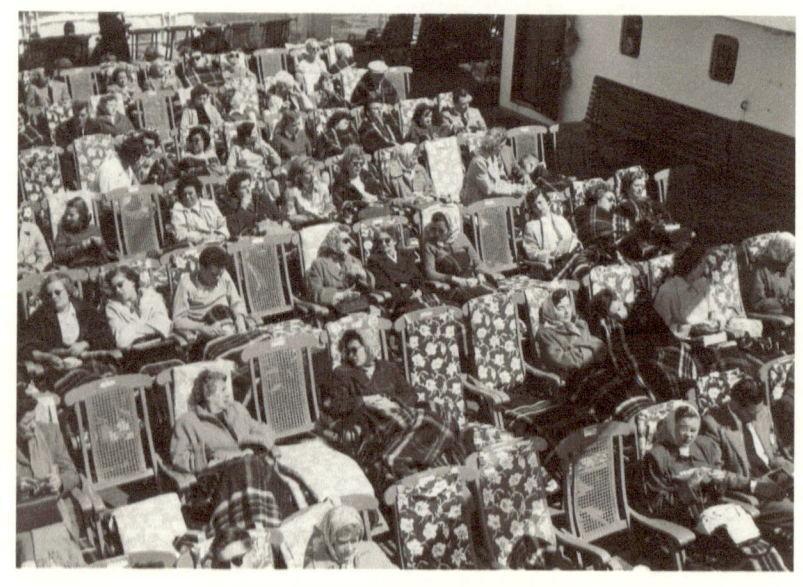

Mother & Phyllis, (ssMaasdam)

George. 1941

Mother when young.

PART TWO

Chapter 12

"Have you ever tried to commit suicide?" The impatient caustic question hung as if in mid-air, whilst my tired and bewildered mind searched wearily over the all too frequent handling of bottles of coloured tablets and capsules. The dazed walking across busy main roads in the path on oncoming traffic, and the swaying dangerously upon the edges of railway platforms.

"No". I replied to the questioner, a largely built, brusque mannered doctor wearing a filthy white coat. An impatient "Humph" transpired. I lay on the long table whilst he examined me, and then conversed with the Sister and nurse as if I was no longer there. Finally, after thoroughly searching through my clothes, I was told to get dressed. I was then led by the nurse through a maze of low ceilinged tunnels which ran throughout the ancient Victorian hospital and into a large ward. Allocating me a bed and locker, the nurse then showed me the adjoining wash-room. It's absolute bareness struck home forcibly. A line of white wash-hand basins covered the entire length of one side of the flag-stoned room, and opposite was a row of toilet cubicles designed for the minimum of privacy. The doors of these cubicles covered only the middle section, the top of the door was missing also the bottom. Inside the cubicles everything had been removed which could,

I suppose upon reflection, have been considered dangerous for suicidal patients. Even the old fashioned chains or handles for flushing the toilets had been taken away, this function was achieved by pressing a brass button on the floor with one's foot. All the windows were covered with iron bars and the doors to the actual ward were locked. The whole atmosphere was more of a prison than a hospital, especially as the bunches of keys jangled noisily from the belts around the waists of the nurses.

The following morning I was taken to see a Psychiatrist. It was a woman and she was most kind and patient with me. We made no headway however, as like all the other patients in the ward, I had become morose and silent. The shock of finding myself in such a terrible place was hard to overcome. I'd had no idea it was going to be like it was, the Out-Patient Department had been different entirely, and the staff very kind, friendly, and helpful.

Several days passed by with the routine of almost uneatable meals, the constant watching of every movement the patients made by the nurses, and after each meal the counting and checking of the cutlery, before everyone was allowed to leave the bare wooden dining tables. All tablets were issued by the Sister who made sure that they were indeed actually swallowed by the patient whilst she watched, so that there was no chance of anyone collecting them and taking an overdose. The spiteful, sarcastic Sister was hard to bear, as were the bored and uninterested nurses. Each patient was made to feel nothing more than a complete nuisance to the staff.

After several sessions with different psychiatrists I was moved to another ward. This one was a little better although it was even farther down the tunnels of the hospital. There weren't any bars on the windows, although the ward door was still locked, and the precautions regarding pills and cutlery were the same. The ward was large and contained numerous women patients all like myself suffering with depression. Here, as in the other ward, there were strict rules against laying or sitting on the beds during the day. We arose at six o'clock, washed and dressed, and breakfasted at seven-thirty.

I stayed in this ward for two or three days, still with the characteristic unfeeling nursing staff, when the doctors decided to give me E.C.T. (Electro Convulsive Therapy. This consisted of an electric shock to the brain , and appeared to be used when the doctors thought that they could not effect an alternative cure. The treatment had been used for well over thirty years or more, and very few people had benefited from it. Some medical people are convinced that it does more harm than good.) The rest of the patients in the ward were also to be given E.C.T., and although I had previously received it as an out-patient without success, the doctors were determined to try yet again.

Two days a week therefore at nine o'clock in the morning, all the beds in the ward were pulled out into a wide corridor and lined up as closely as possible. All food and dink had been banned from the previous night because of the anaesthetic. Nurses busily examined each patient to remove false teeth and tight garments, if any. We were then placed into the beds which had been reversed. Portable screens were used, and as the medical staff began giving the treatment at one end of the row of beds, they gradually worked their way along moving the screens with them, creating fear and tension amongst the patients as they came. Although I had had the treatment before, like the others I was still terrified, so every patient reached across and held the next patient's hand tightly for comfort until the screens engulfed them. When my turn came I was confronted by a doctor, anaesthetist, Sister and nurse. The needle was inserted into my hand, and to ensure that they didn't start too soon, I talked continuously until the drug worked and everything faded away.

Sometime later I was awakened and the protecting sides of the bed lowered. I remember feeling terrible. My head was absolutely bursting, the room swimming, and a feeling of nausea overpowering. All the patients were then given a cup of tea and a biscuit. That is, until one day one of them happened to choke slightly, then this refreshment was quickly discontinued. The course of this treatment consisted of eight operations, usually two per week. At the end of which a number of the patients decided that they were feeling a little better and were discharged. Unfortunately once again the E.C.T. had not had the slightest affect upon me, however, eager and determined to leave the hospital I pretended to be alright and was also discharged.

Upon returning home I did my utmost to do what all my family and friends advised, "Snap out of it", "Pull yourself together".This was easier said than done, but I returned to work in an endeavour to get back to normal. I saw the Company's doctor and the Personnel Officer, then amongst many unkind whispers and remarks from the staff regarding mental hospitals making me feel most uncomfortable and conspicuous , returned to my department.

I still had a responsible position in a large Export Sales office dealing with all the documentation appertaining to the sale and export of drugs, chemicals, photographic and plastic products. I had started work at the age of fourteen and now in my early thirties , unmarried from choice, and the youngest member of a large family I was still living with my elderly widowed mother. We both got on extremely well together and I loved her dearly. The rest of the family visited fairly often including my closest sister Elsie and her husband Bob from America.

After my spell in hospital I tried very hard to settle down again at home and in my job, but my depression simply got worse. Mother couldn't understand it at all although she tried to help. Following long spells of crying in the firm's cloakroom, shops, supermarkets and at home for no apparent reason, I suffered yet another breakdown and was hospitalized in the same place as before. This time I was not admitted to the 'suicide ward' , although the fear was uppermost in my mind, but into the one from which I was discharged. I now had a male Psychiatrist. Plenty of discussions and yet more E.C.T., all without any noticeable signs of improvement. In the ward there were still locked doors, and bunches of keys jangling at the nurses waists. Nothing had changed. Unfeeling, impatient staff who laughed aloud at patient's various misfortunes, or problems. It was also quite a normal occurrence to see frail, elderly women patients on their hands and knees scrubbing the stone floors of the wards and corridors. Mother came frequently to visit me and quickly fell foul of the peremptory Sister by insisting that if she ever found or heard of me scrubbing the floors there would be trouble. My firm's Personnel Officer also came frequently to visit me.

I made many friends amongst the patients who, as I have always been a good listener, told me all their problems and I helped them as much as I could, when they requested my advice. (I've always been a kind of "Agony Aunt" and even when people come to visit me with help, they end up pouring out all their own troubles and I do my best to help them out with my advice, good or not as the case may be.) One patient Ivy, young, attractive and married with two small children was extremely 'house proud'. With her husband she lived in a beautiful bungalow on a very desirable estate. Proud and happy with all her lovely furniture and so forth she was always cleaning and polishing., When her first baby came along she naturally experienced some difficulty coping with everything, but managed. However, with the arrival of the second child it appeared to her to be quite impossible and it broke her heart to see her once beautiful home becoming untidy and littered. So she sank into depression and ended up in the hospital for treatment. Once she realized and accepted that she could cope by putting her family first and not be so terribly 'house proud', she felt much better and discharged herself. I visited her bungalow for afternoon tea some months later and she was doing well. Her two little boys were delightful.

Alice, a highly strung and very nervous woman endeavoured to remain at my side all the time and just would not leave me. She was married with grown up twin daughters. Her husband couldn't, or wouldn't, try to understand her depression and continually threatened to leave her. We corresponded for several months after our hospital discharge, and I was pleased to hear that they were still together and she was doing well. A woman I really did feel sorry for was Doris. She was rather simple minded, had a pock-marked face and a 'dumpy' figure. She was unfortunately homeless and said that that was the only reason she was in the hospital. To earn her keep she carried out numerous routine tasks for the nurses, and was allowed out to go shopping. She was very friendly and when asked, purchased some sugar and packets of tea for Ivy and me with which we made a huge pot of tea every night for the patients which was most welcome, charging a penny per cup to cover the cost of the ingredients. I don't know what eventually happened to Doris as she was still in the hospital when I left, but like to think they found her a home somewhere.

Chapter 13

At home depression continued to plague me for several years and I spent more time as an out-patient at a local hospital being treated by the same Psychiatrist as before. At the end of one consultation he suggested that I brought two of my closest relatives with me on my next appointment. This I did bringing mother and my brother Fred. He explained to them that he could do no more for me and suggested a brain operation, namely a Leucotomy. We were shocked. He suggested that we got a second opinion first, which we did by obtaining an appointment with a world known Psychiatrist. Supposedly an extremely clever man who was frequently broadcasting on the media, and had in fact written many books. After a short discussion this Psychiatrist laughed at the idea of a Leucotomy, maintaining that he could soon effect a cure for my depression with Insulin Sleep Treatment.

Within a few days of this consultation I received a letter of admittance to the Waterloo Women's Hospital. When I arrived I discovered that one ward only was for the mentally ill, and the difference between this hospital and the previous one was absolutely amazing. The ward itself was brightly decorated, had unlocked doors, and there were no bars on the windows. Beautiful indoor plants and flowers were everywhere. There was one large room and several smaller ones for no more than two patients. The food was plentiful and delicious, and there wasn't any counting of cutlery or jangling keys . Most of all there was a happy, laughing, caring and understanding nursing staff. I found it all hard to believe after the conditions in the previous hospital and had to pinch myself to ensure that I wasn't dreaming.

I was placed into the large room and put to sleep for eight weeks. The doctors used Insulin and of course my 'old friend' E.C.T. I recall awaking quite often and talking to a nurse sitting at the side of my bed. She continuously 'shushed' me because of the other sleeping patients. I'd always suffered with insomnia and this even troubled me with this treatment. Also, one problem I experienced with E.C.T. was a badly bitten mouth. At the end of the eight weeks sleep treatment mother told me that every time she had visited me my mouth had been bruised and swollen.

The famous Psychiatrist saw me several times. He was always followed by a large contingent of students which I found quite off-putting. He wasn't happy with my condition and prescribed special anti-depressant tablets. Whilst taking these I had to carry a card with me which had to be produced to GP's, dentists, pharmacists and so forth., There was also a large food restriction. Even gravy and cheese were banned, and the diet was extremely difficult to adhere to. I was told that cheese alone could kill me whilst taking these tablets. I never attempted to verify this statement....

When I returned to work after my discharge from the hospital I saw the company's doctor once more. She suggested that I now took a rehabilitation course and that she would make all the arrangements. Mother was quite happy about this, so once again I packed my suitcase and set off this time accompanied by the firm's welfare officer. This time we travelled from Victoria station to Sussex. The only other occupant in the carriage was a dark haired, slimly built man, who was about the same age as myself. The elderly lady welfare officer took the opportunity to doze off, and the man kept staring across at me trying and hoping for some conversation but I ignored him and watched the passing scenery. When we arrived at our destination a mini bus was waiting for us outside the station. I impulsively kissed the welfare officer as a thank you for her company and boarded the vehicle along with several other train passengers, one of these being the man from my carriage. (Who at a later stage told me that because I had kissed the woman goodbye, he thought that she was my mother.)

After travelling for roughly about fifteen minutes the mini bus drew up outside the most beautiful Tudor mansion. Upon walking up the steps and through the front door, we found ourselves in a large hall with highly polished oak floors, preceding a lovely wide staircase with a curved balustrade. A number of people entitled 'Pre-fects' awaited and welcomed us, then showed us to our bedrooms. Mine I discovered was on the first floor. The room contained in all, eight single beds with adjacent lockers and there was a small wash-hand basin. A little farther along the corridor there was a large well equipped bathroom. The rest of the female travellers entered and chose their beds. The one next to mine was taken by a pretty dark haired girl and we quickly became friends. It was an instantaneous and permanent friendship which survives mainly through correspondence to this very day. As I recall, another young girl entered the bedroom with us, took one look around the room, picked up her suitcase, left the room and we never saw her again.

We discovered that all the male residents were accommodated on the ground floor of the building and were never allowed anywhere near the women's quarters, although both sexes mixed freely below. There were a number of rooms downstairs, one of which was kept strictly for the men. They called it the Billiard room but used it mainly as a retreat from female company. There was no television or radio at the centre, but there was a large ballroom furnished with dart-boards, table tennis tables, an old upright piano, and walled by numerous straight-backed wooden chairs. The dining room was quite spacious also. Meals had to be collected at the counter upon entry, and dirty dishes returned afterwards. At one end of the dining room there was a raised platform upon which the staff had their meals. In a corner just inside the main entrance of the manor there was another staircase. This was narrow and almost unnoticeable, probably used by servants in previous times.

We, the new arrivals, were given a meal before retiring at approximately ten o'clock. We had also been presented with our own individual dinking mugs with our names clearly printed on the outside. I was the first one up in the morning and we all breakfasted at eight. After breakfast we, the newcomers were assembled in the dining room and issued with exercise books containing all kinds of weird and wonderful puzzles. Personally I had great difficulty understanding them, and haven't seen anything like them since. I did the best I could at deciphering them however, in the allotted time. Afterwards we were all shown around the beautifully kept grounds of the manor including two out-buildings. One of them was used for gardening purposes, the other for hobbies and physical training.

Several days passed and although it was early in the year and quite chilly, my new friend Pat and I would, soon after breakfast, go for long walks through the grounds and out into the lovely countryside. As much as we could in our present frame of minds, we both thoroughly enjoyed these walks.

Alas, one morning just as we were venturing out, we were stopped and told that we were supposed to look at the rosta on the notice board first thing every morning for our daily instructions. Obediently, we did this and discovered that we had been allocated doctor appointments and also various other tasks to perform. Thus our delightful morning walks were then terminated.

Gardening jobs appeared on the notice board for both Pat and I most of the time, and we were instructed upon our duties in the gardening building daily. Our most frequent job was the transplanting of hundreds of tiny seedlings into boxes, presumably for sale outside although we were never told what happened to them. It was of course a very simple and monotonous task and we soon became bored. There was no supervision and we worked at our own speed. We discovered that the heavy gardening duties were carried out by the male patients. Other small tasks which we, together with the other female patients performed, was laying the tables for meals, clearing them, and making the evening drinks. We worked alongside the men making sandwiches for supper, and so forth. The washing up however, was done by the male patients who were the only ones allowed to operate the huge dishwasher, in case of accidents. All the duties were carried out in a light hearted manner amidst much chatter and good humour. The patients were an extremely friendly crowd and got on well together. Some encouragement was given by the staff to join in the hobby and physical recreation classes but Pat and I were not particularly interested in these activities, and declined.

My name appeared on the notice board fairly quickly with an appointment to see a specified doctor and I was instructed to use the narrow winding staircase for this somewhat dubious pleasure. Upon entering the designated room I was quite surprised to see a black and brown dirty looking mongrel laying stretched comfortably out on the examination couch. I sat down on a chair in front of a large cluttered desk, behind which sat a burly, middle-aged, white haired man. He had a very red face and rather a bull dog look about him. Introducing himself as Dr. Harris he thereupon shouted several questions at me, and as I refused to reply because of his bad mannered attitude, swore a number of times instructing me to swear back at him. He even suggested that I hit him with a ruler or something else handy from his desk, anything but sit there in silence. I was amazed at his attitude. He grew more and more vehement, and it made me dislike him intensely. Apart from requesting help with my insomnia problem, I continued to remain silent. He was certainly no gentleman in any sense of the word! This kind of doctor interview continued all the time I was at the centre. I was however, prescribed a sleeping pill which I discovered was useless because it was so mild it had no affect whatsoever. I had to obtain this pill by joining a queue of patients outside the Sister's office every night. I got no sleep all the time I was there except for one night when the Sister was off duty and the nurse gave me two stronger pills warning me not to say anything about the matter.

Chapter 14

The men and women at the centre quickly appeared to make attachments, my friend Pat also had one or two boyfriends whilst she was there. She was with one of them one evening and I was in the dining room alone collecting my evening dink of cocoa, when I found that the only vacant seat was at a table next to the man who was in my railway carriage when I travelled down to the centre. He greeted me and leaned across the table offering me a 'welsh cake' from a small tin in his hand, telling me that his sister had made them for him. I gratefully accepted and we exchanged a few words. Gradually during the next few weeks we became rather friendly. His name was John. A quiet and serious looking man who was apparently very lonely. He taught me how to play darts, and we played table tennis, not that I was any good at either game. My interest and real pleasure in sport had been playing court tennis. On Sunday mornings John and I got the ballroom ready for the church services. Unfortunately we were the only two patients who attended these services, and I don't think that the Vicar was any too pleased after coming to the centre to take them.

John and I, like the other patients, went out together in the late afternoon and early evenings. The centre had a curfew of seven- thirty pm. Most of the others went to a nearby public house, but we went for walks along the country lanes. Once or twice we went into a small village Inn for a Lager or Tomato juice and listened to taped music played by the landlord. It was a quaint old-fashioned place and never crowded. In fact, usually we were the only two people there at that time of the evening. Neither of us were drinkers, but we enjoyed the peaceful rustic atmosphere.

Apparently all the patients at the centre had a variety of problems. Pat told me that she was a 'compulsive eater'. She said that the doctor at the centre laughed at her when she explained and told her "to let her skirts out". Naturally she was quite upset about this, it certainly wasn't at all helpful. John it seemed suffered from mild depression and his firm had sent him to the centre because of continuous absences from work. He told me that he had the same doctor there as I did, but unlike me got on very well with him. Bill, an extremely likeable middle-aged man, who was always witty and jolly, said that he had been sent to the centre by his GP and told that he was going there for convalescence. He had quite a shock! Another friendly elderly man there suffered severely with Parkinson Disease, and was very, very, shaky on his feet. He used two walking sticks to get about. The doctor he saw at the centre told him to throw away his sticks and run around the grounds. A young man was advised to get drunk and forget all about his problems. He did just that at the nearby Public house and ended up in a ditch covered in mud. The rest of the men pulled him out and got him back to the centre, where once again sober, he discovered that his troubles weren't cured at all. It all appeared to be quite ludicious. So we all did our best to help each other.

A 'Tramp's Ball' was held at the centre one night and everyone went overboard dressing up , dirtying their faces, clothes, and endeavouring to out do each other with their ideas. Pat and

John joined in with the festivities but as I did not particularly care for parties, especially at that time, I disappeared upstairs out of the way of the noise and crowds. They told me the following morning that they'd all thoroughly enjoyed themselves. It was the only entertainment put on at the centre whilst we were there.

It was shortly after that I had met John in the dining room and we had become friends, only about a week, when Pat found me in the grounds and told me that he'd informed her that he was going to marry me. We both laughed at this idea and found it quite amusing, poor John. I never mentioned the conversation to him though as I didn't want to embarrass him, or hurt his feelings.

Pat and I didn't bother to go gardening as instructed one day as I was suffering from one of my crying bouts. We walked around the grounds instead and she did her best to comfort, and buck me up. We accidentally bumped into Bill there who appeared to be very concerned. He suggested that I dry my tears altogether and go into Brighton with him for the day. I flatly refused his kind offer, but he and Pat both talked me into going. Bill and I then slipped out of the centre and took the bus. We didn't get as far as Brighton but ended up in Guildford. There we saw a good film at a cinema and dined at an expensive restaurant. It was a most pleasant and enjoyable outing and we both enjoyed it. When we returned to the centre Pat met us at the door and told us that our absence hadn't been noticed by the staff. She did say however, that John had been very annoyed about our outing when she'd told him and he'd disappeared into the Billiard room to sulk. He stayed in there until an amused Bill went in and brought him out. It appeared that John possessed a very jealous nature. This incident amused Bill so much that, purely out of devilment I'm sure, he made a great effort to be at my side for the remainder of our stay.

I really liked Bill and enjoyed his company. After meals when the four of us, Pat, John, Bill and I sat talking together, Bill and I often indulged in a kind of harmless pretence. Between us we likened the centre into a kind of prison camp and invented various ways of tunnelling out, past imaginary vicious guard dogs, and the inevitable sentries. John and Pat never joined in or commented about our strange ideas. They just left us to our fantasies. They both probably thought that Bill and I were a little bit crazy at times, and I expect we were. Vivid imaginations!

One morning instead of being sent to perform allotted tasks we were all told to go into the ballroom and once there were given many more strange puzzles to decipher. On this occasion we were timed by an elderly, guant faced man blowing a tinned whistle, once to commence, and once again to finish. I like the others was then taken to another doctor, told to lay on a couch while leather headgear and pulse attachments were applied. I was left alone for a short time before being released by the same doctor. Then I was sent back to the ballroom with the other patients to do more puzzles, timed as before by the elderly gentleman with the tin whistle. No one bothered to explain what it was all about, or if anything had been achieved or discovered by this exercise. To this day it still remains an unsolved mystery.

The whole time that we were at the centre, it being early in the year, the weather was bad. There was plenty of rain, snow, and gale force winds. The latter bringing down one of the giant trees along the driveway to the manor, which barred all incoming and outgoing traffic until it was sawn into logs and cleared away. I actually watched it from an upstairs window as it crashed to the ground and it was quite frightening. Luckily no one was hurt. Some time afterwards when the weather was a little better, Pat, John, and I obtained permission and went into Brighton for the day by bus. Although it was very cold and the town rather deserted, we had quite an enjoyable time, and returned to the centre in plenty of time for curfew.

It appeared though that nothing would shift my persistent depression and my crying spells continued. I was seen by Dr. Harris and he said that they could do no more for me, (not that they had done anything!). So I said goodbye to everyone and went home. Dr. Harris laughed before I left the centre, shook me by the hand, and said "Don't forget to send me a piece of wedding cake." Astounded, my reply of "You'll be lucky." was met with, "I think we all will."I gathered from this that John had been telling the doctor about his feelings for me, and I was very annoyed.

John and Pat both left the centre on the same day as me. John returned to his lodgings in London, Pat to her home in the country. However, we all kept in touch with each other, Pat through her letters and John by visits and occasional weekends at my home. After only a few of these visits for some unspecified reason, mother took a dislike to John and would no longer allow him into the house. I still met him and accompanied him to concerts, operas, cinemas, and theatres. He was always a gentleman, and as with other boyfriends I kept the friendship strictly platonic.He, I'm afraid wanted nothing else but for us to become engaged, but accepted friendship and companionship hoping that I would change my mind at a future date.

Chapter 15

When I returned to work I was offered the chance of promotion to a junior executive in the same department. In the hope that a change would be the answer to my depressive problem I took the promotion. I experienced no difficulty at all with the job and carried on doing it for several months before I had to give in once again. Depression it seemed, was a relentless foe. I returned to the London hospital as an out-patient, had many more wretched E.C.T.'s , and a course of monthly injections, the ingredients of which were never disclosed. During this period of time I had many falls both inside and outside my home, sustaining a number of minor injuries, and much embarrassment when it happened outside in the street or in public places.

After about a year of prolonged absences the Personnel Officer of the company visited me at home and told me that regrettably they would have to let me go. She gave me a cheque for £250 which included the money for the twenty-five years length of service gold watch. Her whole attitude was one of concern and regret, and she added the comments that the company had instructed her to inform me that they would be only too pleased to have me back again, if in six month's time I obtained a doctor's certificate to confirm that my health had improved. When she finally left, I felt a great sense of relief that I no longer had to worry about all the time being off sick, and being an obligation to my employer.

Mother, by this time was really getting on in years and was glad to have me home as she needed much more assistance and attention. Due however, I am convinced to the innumerable E.C.T. treatments, I found that I could no longer think very clearly and my head continually felt like 'a block of wood'. My power of concentration, once so wonderful, had completely disappeared, and my powerful memory was sadly lacking. I did the best that I could in the circumstances and took over all the household chores , and shopping etc., (although I always returned home from the shops in tears, for no apparent reason), and generally looked after the two of us. I began to 'eat for comfort' and put on quite a lot of bodily weight. One particularly bad fall I had during this time caused me to be rushed into hospital by ambulance for X-rays and examinations. The two ambulance men, upon seeing the state of mother and myself, remarked loudly that it was apparently a case of "the blind leading the blind". Luckily, no serious damage had been caused and to my relief, I was allowed to return home. Mother no longer spent most of her time machining but took up knitting and became most proficient in it. I also bought her many complicated Jig-saw puzzles which gave her a lot of pleasure, and when I visited the local library I always brought some of the large text books home with me showing pictorial views of the countryside and antiques for her to see. Television was also greatly enjoyed by mother although her hearing had badly deteriorated and I found that I had to spend a lot of time explaining everything that had happened in various scenes. By the time I had finished one scene, the next had almost gone. Mother and I went for a walk everyday into a local park and we both enjoyed the fresh air, we even went into the park together during the cold winters when the lake was frozen over and we were the only people there. We both had a dream or fantasy of running our own little shop or business, and every Friday evening I spent hours wading through the adverts in Dalton's Weekly and the Exchange & Mart., with of course no possible material benefit because of financial requirements. I recall during this time that mother hugged me to her very often and of all things, thanked me. I kept telling her not to be so foolish, I didn't want or deserve any thanks. She also frequently told me to go and get married, I think she was now secretly worried that I would eventually be left on my own.

Because we were still not on the telephone I, as I had done many times in the past, tried again to teach mother how to use the corner telephone box, but as she was still nervous and rather afraid of using a telephone at all she vied away from it altogether. I always thought it would be a good idea for her if, and when, there might be an emergency, but she wasn't at all interested. Too frightened altogether of the machine.

Continuing to attend St. Thomas's Hospital in London , (the Waterloo hospital had closed like many other hospitals by then), I saw numerous doctors who in turn prescribed different tablets and injections to no avail. Their continuous diagnosis was as before, "A severe inferiority complex". Every day became a new struggle. I prayed nightly that I would die in my sleep and that there would be no tomorrow. Poor mother who didn't understand the problem at all, did her best to comfort me and repeatedly told me "to count my blessings". Secretly I hoarded up tablets, but mother's obvious reliance upon me stopped me from taking them. George, my eldest half-brother, took me aside and told me that she lived only for my sake, and that I must live for her. He obviously k new what I had in mind. Married, like the rest of the family, he always had dinner with mother and I twice weekly after work. When he died suddenly from a heart attack, it broke mother's heart. She just could not accept it. I remember having to cradle her in my arms night after night for many weeks while she cried like a baby. I cried too of course, but must admit that selfishly as well, many of my tears were because it wasn't me that the Lord had taken. Mother appeared never to completely recover from his death.

Members of the family continued to visit from time to time, including Elsie and Bob who flew in from America. Alec and family didn't visit very often as they lived some distance away. (We always thought that Alec must have had some 'gipsy' blood in his veins as he was always selling up and moving around the country. We never knew where he would be next. He was a bit of a wanderer.) Fred, and Edith's husband Peter had become involved with the Union and were now Union Secretaries working in the offices. Fred and Lillian had divorced and Fred had married again to Marian, who I understand worked with him. Lillian took custody of the three children. Bella and Jim still lived quite near us. She worked in a motor car factory as a machinist, and we saw her fairly often. Sometime later when the Pre-fabricated houses were demolished, they were put into a flat and Bella hated it so they moved into the country near Burnham-on-Crouch, a yachting place I love.

In 1976 the country was swallowed up by a terrible drought in the summer. Elsie and Bob I remember came over from America on a visit and on one occasion accompanied me to the West End to meet John. The four of us spent the day there together and enjoyed ourselves. I recall all the green lawns in the Royal Parks had withered and turned brown with the heat and lack of rain. We even managed though to row out on one of the slightly diminished lakes, I should say the men did the rowing, and we just sat back and trailed our fingers in the water. Elsie, I remember took me aside later and told me that John really thought the world of me. I can't think why! It was always so wonderful to see Elsie and Bob and quite sad when they left.

Bella had bought three or four chalets near the sea-side town of Clacton where she spent a lot of her time. When mother was ninety-one years old in 1977, both of us had a very pleasant week in one of them as we had on previous occasions. We went for our usual walks along the sea-front, walks that mother always enjoyed. Naturally she needed my assistance and could now walk only slowly. Mother appeared to be so very fit in herself that I was most surprised when she became ill at the end of September that year. She suffered from severe diarrhoea and sickness and our new African G.P. (Dr. Dean had died of a heart attack) refused to visit her when I asked him on the telephone. Because of his refusals I had to go along to the surgery where I told him exactly what I thought about his neglect. I can remember saying that "he wouldn't treat an animal that way", and he wasn't all that pleased. However, he came out to the house and treated mother who responded well and was soon up and about again. I had always been so quiet and well-mannered that because of my surgery outburst, the doctor then labelled me quite incorrectly as a Schizophrenic. Unfortunately, no doubt this was written into my medical file as well. (I had always been taught to regard doctors and the medical profession with a great deal of respect and a little awe as persons of a far higher 'plane' .)

A few weeks later poor mother fell ill again. This time it was far more serious as she experienced great difficulty eating. She ate very little, sometimes nothing at all and was up all night, every night, in the freezing cold bathroom vomiting, or trying to. I did everything I could to look after her. Gave her milk puddings, soups, yoghurts, and even substances like Complan, but mother could not keep anything at all down. Fred took her by car to attend a number of hospital appointments, but it was some time before I learned that mother had Cancer of the

Oesophagus and had only another three, or at the most, six months to live. It was a terrible shock., The only reassuring fact was that she appeared to be in no pain, and although very weak from lack of nourishment, and feeling the cold badly which she had never done before, mother never complained once. She was a wonderful person. At this time I found that I could not cry at all and just had a terrible painful ache in my chest. Mother and I never spoke about her illness, or what it was, and I still don't know if she knew what she was suffering from or if she ever discussed it with any other member of the family. They never said and I did not ask.

Eventually the hospital supplied mother with small bottles of different flavoured glucose drinks, which I must say I had great difficulty getting her to take. Fred brought various home made invalid meals for her made by his wife Marian, but she couldn't eat them. Mother just grew weaker and weaker as the days went by , and all she wanted to do was to sit and doze by the fireside on the settee clasping me by the arm for comfort. She would somehow lock my arm with her own, and I had great difficulty mentally and physically, leaving her to do the various household chores. Every afternoon about four o'clock Edith and Peter would call in on their way home from work. They were now involved with council work, both being Councillors, and they would simply sit themselves down in the armchairs and talk happily about council business. Mother did not particularly want or enjoy these visits, neither did I. One day she was taken by Fred for her hospital appointment and never returned. I spent the whole day pacing the floor wondering what had happened and was worried stiff. After a while Fred returned home with mother's clothes and said that the hospital had admitted her and were feeding her with a drip-tube. He told me quite firmly that when I saw her I mustn't cry because of seeing any tubes etc., that they may be using on her.

We went every day to visit her. She had been placed in an accident ward which was terribly crowded with patients of all age groups suffering from various complaints. Mother I am sure that, although she did not like being in hospital at all, would have been a lot happier in a ward with patients of a similar age. She was so terribly unhappy. She had a drip-tube fitted in her hand and complained that she had to take the complete drip-tube stand with her even when she went along to the toilet, which was more difficult for her as she was so weak. Mother also said that she was forced to sit on a chair by the side of her bed all day in the freezing cold until the heating was eventually turned on at visiting times. As I mentioned earlier, mother was not the type to complain at all. Every time I visited her she begged me to give her the bus fare home. Each day she became more and more unhappy and even threatened to walk home on her own, which was of course impossible in her condition. Mother's persistent wish to come home and request for the bus fare broke my heart even more than ever. The loneliness of the house also became unbearable, although each time mother asked I told her that everything was fine and I was doing alright. I no longer bothered to go upstairs to bed at night but sat on the settee in front of the fire. After several days and nights this way I was finding it almost impossible to move around much at all, my limbs became so stiff. It was a terrible effort to make myself a cup of tea. At the end of one week like this I found that it was too difficult to visit mother at all on that day. I felt terrible about this but simply couldn't control my lower limbs properly at all. The rest of the family told mother, when she asked where I was, that I had a bad cold. As I was always a sufferer of Sinusitis etc., upon having a cold mother never queried this excuse. One morning a few days later, Fred and Edith called at the house and told me that mother had died in her sleep. I hadn't even had the chance to say goodbye.

Several days passed and members of the family gathered at the house for mother's funeral, John also arrived. I could do nothing. Elsie and Bob arrived from America and they did their very best to comfort me and gave me a lot of support. I really don't think that I'll ever get over the feeling of guilt that I deserted mother when she needed to see me so much that last time before she died. I was ready to attend the funeral with the others but Bella very forcefully said "You're not going." I did not feel up to disobeying her. She was a very dominant person. So regretfully up to this very day I didn't attend mother's funeral. John stayed at home with me but his constant chatter about what he'd bought his nephews for Christmas at such a time was extremely annoying, and I just had to ignore it all.

The whole family appeared to celebrate the funeral in grand style, much to my disgust. I was so terribly upset I found their attitude difficult to understand and accept. I expect that they were just as upset but managed to hide their feelings. They were all obviously very annoyed that mother had left everything that she had, which wasn't very much at all, to me. Elsie and Bob stayed with me a further two weeks after the funeral before returning to America, during which time Elsie and Bella accompanied me on my now routine visit to St. Thomas's hospital, and it was suggested by Bella that I was admitted, but I declined. The Vicar from the local church called in at home to see me several times whilst Elsie and Bob were still with me, until he realised that he wasn't achieving anything at all. He spent too much of his time talking to Bob and discussing American football, besides drinking endless cups of tea. I was glad when he stopped the visits. When Elsie and Bob left, Bella and her husband Jim came to stay from Southminster for two weeks. After which I was alone once more in an empty house. I went back again to sitting on the settee every night instead of going upstairs to bed, and not bothering about getting anything to eat at all. A week or more passed slowly by, before the doorbell rang and when I opened the door I found it was Bella's daughter Eileen. We had a cup of tea and a talk and she was very concerned about me so she sent for my doctor who once again did not visit, but prescribed more pills for a nervous breakdown. Eileen then called around to Edith's house which was only ten minutes distance away and told her how worried she was about me. Edith and her husband Peter were both local Councillors and after (unknown to me at the time), discussing with the rest of the family whether or not to put me into a mental hospital, found room for me in a Physically Handicapped Home for a temporary stay of, they said two weeks. That was the arrangement as far as I was informed. In fact however, I remained in the Home for two whole years.

Chapter 16

During these two years I still found life very difficult. At first I would sit silently in the lounge staring down at the carpet beneath my feet praying that I would die. At visiting time one day one of the women residents asked her husband to have a word or two with me and try to cheer me up. He did, and after a few visits we became friends. The old adage however, of looking at someone far worse off than yourself was to me then entirely false. There were approximately twenty handicapped residents in the Home which was well staffed with domestics, attendants, a Matron, and her deputy. The majority of these residents were in wheelchairs, some of them electrically run. I soon discovered that many of them expected to be waited on hand and foot, although quite capable of doing things for themselves. They appeared to carry large 'chips' on their shoulders, and hadn't fully accepted their disabilities.. So, being physically fit myself, they all immediately started ordering me to do everything for them. Fully sympathetic with their problems I helped all I could. We were all expected to live together like one big happy family, which didn't quite work out because of jealousies, spitefulness, and continual arguments. The atmosphere was always electrically charged and one never knew quite what to expect from one day to the next. It was not a happy place at all although modern and quite well equipped.

The matron was nearly at retirement age. She was rather aloof and quite withdrawn, but very strict and was avoided by both staff and residents if at all possible. She confessed quite briskly that she had no idea at all of how to treat anyone suffering from Depression, so with the blessing and prompting of both Edith and Peter chose to make me work as much as possible. All I needed was a cap and apron to be an unpaid member of staff who, taking a lead from the matron, also found me quite a few of their own jobs to do. I went about the Home as if in a trance just doing everything I was told to do and silently praying that death would soon come and take me as a blessed relief. Death did come to two of the residents whilst I was there, one had a Heart Attack, and the other simply starved himself to death.

I had a room on the ground floor along with the other residents. It was very small and furnished with a three foot bed, chair, single wardrobe, and wash-hand basin. Every room, including the toilets and bathroom, were fitted with loud alarm bells for the occupants to use for attention if and when needed. These bells seemed to be ringing continuously night and day. I did my own laundry, looked after myself, and kept my room clean and tidy. Most of the residents had their own portable radios, tape recorders, and televisions which blared out their noises from early morning until late at night. On the ground floor there was also a large lounge with comfortable armchairs. Inside a 26" television had pride of place and arguments about programmes were noisy and endless. A few of the residents refused to sit in the lounge at all preferring the privacy of their own small rooms. Others would sit and watch the television until it finished and the white dot appeared on the screen.

I liked all the staff and got on very well with most of them, although many of them were rather lazy and spent quite a lot of time in the staff room smoking, drinking tea or coffee, and chatting., sometimes refusing to come and attend to any of the residents who needed their help, and making them wait. Unlike the matron, her deputy was extremely friendly and life always seemed a little easier when she was on duty. She would join in with the residents, even playing Bingo and other games with them in the evenings., She had rather en engaging personality.

One morning the matron told me that she required my room for a new resident and offered me accommodation in her two bed roomed flat on the first floor. It was a beautiful flat and we got on quite well together while I was there. Noise still bothered me however, and I soon discovered that, perhaps through loneliness, she would habitually have the television and music centre both blaring out and would be machining at the same time. Dressmaking appeared to be her personal passion. (She also had a passion for sunbathing in her bikini on the veranda when it was at all possible, and because of her age looked quite peculiar laying there.)

I was still attending the hospital as an out-patient and because matron did not particularly want to be involved with my health problem, she left me in sole charge of my own tablets and medication., but handled all the other resident's personally. One or two members of my family visited me occasionally, and the other residents had plenty of visitors, most of whom became very friendly towards me. There were a number of parties at the Home whilst I was there, but I usually slipped away as I couldn't stand all the commotion. Also the parties sometimes became rather coarse and vulgar which I hadn't any liking for. The Salvation Army band came to play fairly often and were very enjoyable. Church services were also held in a room at the Home on Sundays. None of the residents liked receiving floral bouquets from the Church next door though as I was told that they came from funerals. I was often asked by the matron to arrange these flowers in vases.

The matron always appeared to be begging for funds for the Home and thinking of ways to obtain donations. She held many jumble sales in which all the residents were involved and I hated all the hassle. I remember thinking at the time that I would never go to a jumble sale again. Every resident had to pay for their board and lodgings according to their financial situations. Matron took my sickness benefit and gave me back £3 a week which I had to use for all my personal requirements which included everything from clothes, toiletries, washing powder, and so forth. So of course I had quite a job to cope, there certainly wasn't any money to spare. Some of the residents paid £70 or £80 per week, not from choice, simply because they could afford it. Most of them obtained Government Mobility allowance.

After a few weeks I was moved once more. This time into a lovely bed-sit next to matron's flat. Apparently the idea was to see how I managed. I loved the bed-sit and was happy there. I wasn't allowed to spend much time in it though as the powers to be thought that I might brood, which was rather sad. I had my old typewriter there with me and really enjoyed my time alone writing. I still had to come down to meals and to mingle with the other residents. Meal times were terrible. Everyone would shout or talk at once. The noise was deafening. At times one or more of the residents would suffer a fit , falling across the table and scattering the food everywhere. My nerves were always badly shattered afterwards and sometimes I would take seven or eight Valium tablets to calm myself down. I would also get on the telephone and talk to the Samaritons or a friend and get some verbal help. Afterwards I would disappear upstairs to my bed-sit, have a good cry, and recover. Whilst I was staying in the bed-sit I had a number of falls and had quite a struggle to pick myself up. I soon discovered that no one was particularly interested in this fact, so like many other things I kept this to myself.

It was extremely difficult to make friends with anyone in the Home because of all the jealousies and arguments. I tried to make friends with one woman only to discover that she was very spiteful, lied continuously, and was a very good actress when the inclination took hold of her. Her husband Tom was a very helpful and friendly man. He visited her often and he and I became firm friends. It was very difficult to hold any kind of conversation with the residents when I felt the urge, which luckily I didn't, at least not very often. I found it much easier to chat to certain members of the staff. Tom often took his wife home with him for weekends, and one day feeling rather more friendly she invited me to accompany them. This I did and had a very nice weekend, it was a welcome change from the Home. I subsequently spent quite a few weekends there, and also visited their daughter who lived in Devon, with them for a week's holiday. During the whole of the two years I spent in the Home not one member of my own family invited me to visit or stay with them at all. Tom also helped me by introducing me to taped music. He gave me a tape recorder with a few tapes and also recorded nearly all my vinyl records on to tapes for me. Tom also lent me an old black and white television, and what with the music as well, the time spent in my bed-sit was even better than ever.

One morning after breakfast we were all still in the dining room about to disperse when the matron came bustling in with a big amused smile on her face waving a bunch of papers in her hand, saying "look everyone, we have a Writer in our midst". She had found my MSS in the bed-sit near my typewriter and brought it over to me who was now the most surprised and surveyed occupant in the room. I was very embarrassed and a little annoyed, especially as she had read my draft through without my knowledge or permission. However, she confessed that she had quite enjoyed reading it and as it was all about my American trip, would I mind lending it to a schoolboy she knew as he was particularly interested in the subject. He was apparently working on a project or something about America for his school. I met the young teenage boy later, he was very nice and pleased to borrow my MSS, returning it at a later date quite happily.

Chapter 17

Whilst staying in the Home a rather bossy woman had a fall from her wheelchair one day and complained that she had hurt her arm. The matron took a look at her arm and insisted that there was nothing at all wrong with it although the woman appeared to be in a great deal of pain. She continued to complain for about three or four more days, so I ordered a taxi and took her to the casualty ward of a local hospital, where she had treatment for a torn ligament. When we returned the matron wasn't at all pleased that we had acted upon our own initiative. Some weeks later the same woman became incontinent and had to buy the protective clothing and pads for herself. She was very depressed about all this, including the cost, and I found her crying in her room. So, I got on the telephone to the welfare department and ordered a supply of incontinent materials. Early the following morning three or four large bundles were deposited outside the front door of the Home, and I of course had to tell the matron exactly what I had done. She was very angry. Later the same day however, she called me, took me aside, gave me a quizzical look, and remarked "You know what Phyllis, I think you could do my job far better than I can", Whether of not this was sarcasm, I wouldn't know. I like to think that she meant it though.

Another incident was that every time I walked along the

corridor downstairs and passed a room marked 'No Entry', I thought I could smell burning. Eventually, I mentioned it to Tom when he was on one of his usual visits. He immediately went to tell the matron saying that the room contained certain electrical equipment and it must be reported as something could be wrong. She telephoned the electricians and they investigated at once and found that there could have been a serious problem, even a fire, as some of the equipment was faulty. Thank goodness I told someone in time even though I was afraid I would find that it was all my imagination.

Time went slowly by and once in the middle of the night laying awake as usual, I discovered that I was virtually paralysed. In my panic, having no telephone or emergency bell in the bed-sit, I had to struggle to move my limbs at all. I had great difficulty trying to sit up and couldn't walk. I was in terrible pain all over my body, especially at the base of my spine. I couldn't even lie or sit down without a great deal of pain. After a while I managed to lie flat on my back for short periods of time for some relief. When she found me like it the matron contacted the London hospital I was attending and they doubled my dosage of anti-depressant tablets. It took several weeks for the aches and pains to disappear, and for me to regain my mobility. During this period of time I was moved to a room downstairs again with the idea of the staff keeping an eye on me. They were unwilling, or unable to do very much for me, in fact I did most of it myself, and in due course returned to my bed-sit. I developed other symptoms such as badly swollen ankles, and severe vertigo. I can't explain the terrible phases of vertigo which were so bad. The rooms, even corridors, swam rapidly around and the floors seemed to come up and meet me. My ears would explode peculiarly and I would have to grab hold and cling frantically to doors, walls, or whatever was near at the time. The hospital then decided to take me off the pills altogether. This had to be done gradually and the dosage was slowly reduced. Two days after finally stopping the tablets altogether I suffered severe withdrawal symptoms. Laying in bed, with my dressing gown on as well, I shook from head to foot, my teeth literally chattering, and I couldn't pull myself together no matter how hard I tried. My doctor immediately put me back on the tablets and after a few days the symptoms completely disappeared. However, I still had swollen ankles and very painful feet which caused me to limp rather badly.

Whilst I was in the Home all the staff went on a week's strike about pay and conditions. That is with the exception of the matron and her deputy. I was given many more tasks to accomplish and all the other residents were instructed to help out as much as they could. Luckily we got a lot of help from outside local volunteers, and although rather disorganised got through the week very well. When the staff returned to work they were none too pleased with our success.

Christmas time many of the residents went home to their families. The few that were left in the Home, including myself, had quite an enjoyable time. It was a lot pleasanter and arguments were temporarily forgotten. There was plenty of Christmas fare and visits from charity organisations. One of these visits was a lorry disguised as a sleigh bearing Father Christmas and his Elves who brought presents for everyone. Carol singers also sang outside the Home under an old-fashioned lamp. On the whole, what with a covering of snow as well, Christmas passed quite nicely that year. Unfortunately however, the Christmas spirit did not last very long and we were soon back to the old way of living, - if you could call it that. In the New Year matron decided to give all the staff and families a party. They all gathered with the residents in the dining room and I was designated to take their coats and outdoor things like a Butler, and also, because after about half an hour matron decided that it was too much for her to make, fetch drinks, and wait on her guests, guess who she nominated to do it? I found myself, a non -drinker with absolutely no knowledge of alcoholic drink of any kind, going around asking people what they'd like and then attempting to supply it, also washing glasses etc., afterwards. My knowledge was so sparse in this, in the end most of them got their own drinks, and all the time matron sat happily by gossiping and enjoying herself.. By the time, which was very late, the party ended I was worn out doing one thing and another when beloved matron decided I should thereupon make plenty of tea for all the residents before they retired. I refused, and told her straight that I'd done enough. Very surprised, she made it herself!

I was still meeting John at the weekends in the West End and we would go to the Albert Hall, and cinemas etc., (I recall that on at least two occasions, after queuing outside a cinema for several hours before obtaining tickets, and then sitting to watch a good film in the warm cinema, I immediately fell asleep. Only awaking when the noise of the audience leaving disturbed me, and feeling quite embarrassed saying dazedly to poor John, "That was very good." The answers I got were a grumpy "How would you know? You slept right through it.") He continually pestered me to marry him however, and finally his persistence wore me down and I agreed to become engaged, but with the proviso that I could change my mind at any time, and so could he. I had no intention of marrying him or anyone else, but accepted the ring we purchased at Hatton Garden simply for the sake of peace. The matron and staff kept nagging at me to name the wedding date, and pressured me by constantly telling me that marriage would be the making of me. I disagreed, so completely ignored their comments. John and I enjoyed each other's company and had similar interests. We both like classical music and concerts, operas, theatres, and good films etc., He did have a terrible obsession with sport and photography which I didn't particularly share, but unfortunately his time keeping was absolutely deplorable. He would keep me waiting for hours then have a feeble excuse. This was a constant bone of contention. He was also I thought, very immature for his age. I don't think that he had any idea of the responsibilities of marriage, and although I had become quite fond of him, I simply did not love him.

As time went by with the help of a friend, namely Tom, I began to regain some self confidence and proceeded to stand up for myself with the staff and residents. I even confronted the matron and told her that I was no longer prepared to be 'an unpaid member of staff', but a resident pure and simple. I recall that she gazed at me so woefully and asked "Whatever has happened to the nice girl who didn't mind what she did?". I continued with a few of my so called duties but refused many others, and gradually everyone got the message. Sometime after this Tom encouraged me to apply for a council flat, which I did. Meanwhile John and I began to quarrel a lot and I broke off the engagement returning his ring. We parted good friends and he said that he would always be there if I needed him.

I eventually obtained a one bed roomed council flat on the same Estate and quite near Tom's house, one which he knew was empty at the time. Feeling rather nervous I left the Home and settled down on my own, after of course giving up my mother's two bed roomed house for which I had continued to pay rent from my savings whilst residing in the Home. (Edith was always there at the Home on time to remind me and request the money for the rent!)

PART THREE

Chapter 18

My flat, which by the way had a lovely fully equipped bathroom, was on the first floor of a block of four on the corner of the road where Tom's three bed roomed house was located, so we lived quite close to each other. As the flat was in poor decorative condition Tom worked very hard in his spare time doing it up. He worked in a local car manufacturing company doing 'shift' work, a fortnight on nights, and a fortnight days. Having no furniture either I stayed mainly at his house until the flat was re-decorated and I had gradually obtained the essentials required to enable me to live there. All the furniture I started off with was of course 'second hand' , and it took many years before I managed to obtain the items I wanted. (When I first moved in I was somehow considered by the council to have been a 'homeless' person and they rallied around and provided me with a few pieces of old furniture to start me off. I was given a very ancient gas stove, a worn rough old dining table, and a couple of wonky dining chairs to match.) Tom helped me a lot by doing all the DIY that was needed, curtain fittings etc., etc., if I needed anything done he was always willing to oblige.In return for his help, and because he lived alone, I spent a great deal of time cleaning his house which was very badly neglected domestically. There were extremely large black cobwebs hanging down from the ceilings everywhere and plenty of dust and grime. I also did the laundry, ironing, mending, and darning etc., and had a meal ready for him when he came home from work. (Even his saucepans and pots were minus their handles - 'typical man living alone'.) I looked after him when he was ill and unable to work as well, and vice versa.

At first when I moved into my flat the surrounding neighbours were all a bit 'stand-offish'. The rumour had gone around, I can't think how, that I had only obtained the flat because my sister was a Councillor. The tenants in the other three flats were all middle-aged couples and as I was single they couldn't understand how I'd got the flat at all. I soon became accepted by two of the occupants but had trouble with the couple in the flat below mine. The man was a retired Sergeant Major and his wife was completely deaf. Derek was the man's name and he possessed a very loud resonant voice. I could clearly hear every word he uttered. He made my life a misery in every way he could. Everything I did, everything I put on my radio or television, he would continuingly comment on adversely, even though I never had the sound on loudly. I recall that one evening I watched the film called 'The Omen', and afterwards when I retired to bed Derek delighted in trying to frighten me with terrible moaning and the sound of clanking chains. I carpeted every room in the flat to keep any noise I might make to a minimum but the comments etc., continued. Finally I complained to the council and was visited by a very nice man who after listening to the problem went down to have a word with Derek. I went with him. After talking to Derek for a little while he told him that he had a disturbingly resonant voice which was clearly heard in my flat, and advised him to lower it, and stop anymore disturbance to me. When he left he told me to live quite normally and happily in my flat and to let him know if I had anymore trouble.

Tom confided to me that he was very unhappily married and had only stayed with his wife because she had contracted Multiple Sclerosis and needed caring for. She was now of course in the Home. He also said that he had never loved her and had only married her during the second world war because she was pregnant by another man, and that he himself was so positive that he would not survive 'D-Day', he'd be giving the child a name and her a 'widow's pension'. Tom did of course survive however, losing only his sense of smell, and carried on with the marriage even though after a very short time he discovered that she was "man hungry". He therefore he said ended up with four children (all married now, two of them with children of their own), three of which were not his. He raised them all and they believed that he was their father, and still do. Upon hearing all this, I of course felt extremely sorry for him, but still continued to endeavour to persuade him to visit his wife in the Home weekly until she died, which he did most reluctantly.

Tom was ten years older than me, and by then I was forty-nine. We became quite closely attached even though we were complete opposites in every way, except for a deep love of animals. He was a supremely confident, domineering, and an almost unstoppably talkative 'rough and ready' London Cockney. He was however, very kind hearted, and would do anything for anybody. Tom helped all his friends and neighbours in every way, they had only to knock at the door and ask and he was there, ready to tackle anything or anyone. He repaired all their vacuum cleaners, lawn mowers, or whatever, and took them back looking almost like new again. (the only problem being that he would do all repairs, as well as some carpentry, and even engines, inside the house including the kitchen and living room. His tools and parts usually spread all around the place, on worktops, sideboards, draining boards, carpets etc., and it was impossible to proceed with anything until he had finished.) Domesticated also, Tom could handle the housework, laundry, and so forth and was an excellent cook especially with cake making. In his entire life he boasted that he had NEVER read a book and thought that it was a complete waste of time reading one, although he always perused his newspaper from the first page to the last. All the children in the street would congregate around his house, forever knocking at the door asking for sweets, cakes, or help with their bicycles as well. There was never a dull moment, and very little peace and quiet.

Tom's family were not all that happy about our association, especially his oldest daughter who appeared to be extremely jealous of our close relationship, and was very much like her "actress" mother, although she did her best to welcome me into her sea-side home when Tom took me there on holiday. None of them wanted to upset their father and tried hard to accept my presence, as I tried very hard to get to like them. We did have some good times on holiday and both enjoyed touring around the Devon country and sea-side. Tom and I also spent several Christmas holidays with his daughter and son-in-law, until we eventually decided to stay at home. Tom's daughter and family enjoyed playing loads of personally written 'puzzles', and a kind of Charades, and would not have the television or radio on at all during Christmas, and both Tom and I were not too keen on these silly games. They were none too happy about having the gas fire on either and it was very cold. They visited Tom and stayed weekends with him quite often. I did meet his eldest son a couple of times but he disappeared altogether from the scene, due I was informed to some kind of family argument, and was not seen by Tom or me for well over twenty years or more. Almost 'The prodigal son'. Tom's youngest son and wife visited occasionally. His youngest daughter lived in Ireland.

I was fifty years old when I eventually lost my virginity, and quite honestly wished that I hadn't bothered. The sexual act meant very little to me I found, and was a lot of terribly embarrassing and unpleasant 'hoo hah' about nothing . A complete waste of time in every way, and I was glad and very relieved when it ended and I could get back to my normal way of life. I discovered that I did not care for sex at all. Thankfully, Tom's and my companionship continued however, and we were partners in every other way and quite often, because we were always seen together everywhere, many people thought that we were man and wife.

Once I was properly settled into my flat with the appropriate furniture we, Tom and I, decided on alternate dinner arrangements. One week I would prepare it in my flat and the following week he would do so in his house. This worked well for a number of years until he was presented with a kitten by his daughter and he felt that it wouldn't be right to leave it on its own during the evenings. From that time on I used to have to go down to his house for dinner every day. (All the bills for groceries etc., were split in half between the two of us as usual). The advent of the kitten also put an end to my holidays with Tom at his daughter's Devon house as he expected me to stay at home and look after the kitten, which I did. (Buster the kitten lived for at least twenty years and both Tom and I loved him dearly. He suffered many illnesses which of course cost a great deal in Veterinary fees but we both took care of those. Unfortunately at the end he had his hind leg broken for the second time and also became incontinent, so sadly we had to have him put to sleep).

One day Tom fell ill with a chest infection. He was unable to go to work and was very poorly so I looked after him. I used to leave my flat every morning at 7.30, collect his newspaper from the corner shop, and let myself into his house, where I would stay all day before returning to my flat in the evening, always making sure to leave him a flask of hot drink before I left. He appeared to get worse instead of better, so I sent for his doctor. Tom's own doctor was, it appeared, away somewhere so he was attended each time I telephoned by emergency doctors who simply prescribed Paracetamol tablets which did no good whatsoever. One doctor did say however, that Tom should not be in a cold bedroom, but in a heated, but airy room. So with the aid of Tom's next door neighbour, I took one of his spare room single beds downstairs into the living room and put him where there was a gas fire, and cared for him there. It took at least eight weeks of constant nursing before Tom recovered. It would have been even longer if his own doctor hadn't finally visited, examined him, told us both that it had been a bad case of Pneumonia, and laughingly said that if he'd been sent to hospital in the beginning, he would have been cured in three or more days. The doctor gave Tom a correct prescription including also a very strong tonic which quickly made him much better. He was visited by some of his family when he was almost well again, but still sleeping in the living room. I remember that his youngest daughter whom I had only met once before, thanked me for taking care of him. Once back on his feet Tom finally took the action that I had already taken in my flat earlier, that of having a gas heater installed in his bedroom, an act which he never regretted. Tom was rather strange in many ways as he would never consider buying anything at all for his own benefit and would prefer to have everyone else's 'left off's' in furniture, and household appliances etc., He always seemed to be happier giving all his money to "his family", (he always earned a good wage), and going without himself even though there were a lot of things he really needed, like for instance a comfortable chair to sit on as he occasionally suffered with back trouble. I would save hard and then buy myself something that I required for my own comfort, or amusement, but before I did Tom would kick up an awful lot of fuss and would argue about the purchase saying that it was completely unnecessary. Afterwards however, within a very short period of time he would usually follow suit and buy himself an identical item, except that is, a decent chair. Tom's family were much better off than he was materially anyway, all having their own properties, and cars etc., even though they were frequently phoning him for money. Tom was, like me, living in council accommodation. He did own an old car, and told me that he'd been driving since he was thirteen, as well as I'm sorry to say, smoking. He did however, manage to give up smoking when he was in his early sixties of his own volition.

Chapter 19

I kept myself very busy with plenty of housework, shopping and cooking etc., during the days but alas unfortunately went down with yet another short burst of depression. This time I spent just two weeks in the local hospital, before discharging myself. The same hospital as before, but this time I was in a small 'lodge' not a ward. In there everyone carried out numerous duties including washing-up loads of crockery after meals and tidying them all into various cupboards. There were only one or two nurses or assistants to supervise, no doctors or Psychiatrists after the initial examination. Whilst I was there Tom visited me every evening upon his return from work, which was good of him and I really appreciated these visits. At a later time I spent a short time at a day hospital and had a brain scan and was told that it had shown that I'd had a lot of minor strokes. (I can't help wondering if they were caused by all those E.C.T.'s I was given, and if that was why I had suffered all those vertigo symptoms and so forth whilst I was in the Home).

My half-sister Bella visited me to see the flat and find out how I was one day, and Elsie and Bob also called in to see me on one of their family visits from America. They were staying with Edith this time as I obviously had no room in my flat for them although I would have loved to have had them with me.

It was wonderful to see them, as it always was. I took them down to Tom's house to meet him, and they stayed to dinner with us, before returning to Edith and Peter's place. Bella's daughter who at that time lived quite nearby, visited Tom and I several times and when Tom was in hospital one time took me to visit him in her car. I never saw my brother Fred and his family after I moved out of our mother's house. For some unknown reason, and I was terribly upset at the time, he wanted nothing more to do with me. Why I just do not know and although I wrote to him and asked, I got no answer at all. As I loved him very much it hit me hard and took some time to get over, but like all things the hurt eventually disappeared and apart from sending Christmas greeting cards to him and family every year, I no longer bother. He, as he apparently wanted, no longer exists now where I'm concerned.

I asked Tom one weekend if he would drive me to the Crematorium where my mother's ashes would have been scattered. He did, and after visiting the office there I discovered the exact place and bought a Plaque to put down in memoriam, also I had her name added into the Book of Remembrance. The gardens there were beautiful and I decided that that was where I would like to have my ashes scattered, close to hers, when I died. Tom took me there to visit the exact place and say a prayer or two for her several times later on.

Quite often on a Sunday Tom would take me to visit his sister Ella and her husband Stanley. We were always made most welcome there. They had an African parrot which they called Joey. He didn't like Tom at all for some reason or other and would show it by dancing up and down on his perch and ruffling his feathers when Tom went near his cage. He was a lovely old thing, the parrot I mean, not Tom. (Although I suppose he wasn't so bad). Both Ella and Stan were very friendly and we appeared to get on well with them. Stan looked a bit like a professor in appearance, and I think that he was quite clever. As a sort of hobby he collected all kinds of things, including second hand domestic appliances and so forth and it was interesting to investigate them all. Tom and I found several items good enough for us to use ourselves and purchased them quite cheaply from him. We were invited to their house for Christmas dinner one year and to Tom's surprise and delight we found his eldest sister there as well. I enjoyed these visits and liked Ella and Stan very much. I was quite upset then when Ella began to have some health problems and after a while was diagnosed as suffering from Alzheimer's disease. As her illness progressed Ella became more and more helpless and was also inclined to wander away if not closely watched. Eventually, she became rather violent as well. Stan was of course very upset and Tom and I helped every way we could. It was very sad when Ella had to go into hospital and died some time later of Pneumonia. After that we lost touch with Stan altogether. Tom was of the opinion that he had gone back to live with his own family, and we never heard from him again.

Tom very happily took early retirement from his firm at the age of sixty two and was given a good pension and large redundancy payment. I had saved enough money for my fare so we both travelled by 'plane to visit Elsie and Bob in the States for a month in the summer of 1982. It wasn't such a wonderful trip by 'plane as it was by ship, and I was extremely nervous and suffered from Claustrophobia being shut up for seven hours. I hated the flight and was glad to reach terra firma again. Tom on the other hand, loved it and never wanted to land. Elsie and Bob were delighted to see us and we were made very welcome of course, although they were both working at the Veteran's hospital during the daytimes. We both managed to get around, see the sights, and visit Elsie in the Veteran's restaurant at lunchtimes and meet a few of the patients there. Some of them were so badly disabled due to injuries suffered in the war that it was quite upsetting to see them. We visited one of the hospital open days with Elsie, Bob and their grandchild Debbie, and it was wonderful and extremely interesting. I bought a few of the handicrafts made by the patients which I really admired to put in my flat when I came home, and still have them now. Upon my insistence, on another day Tom and I visited a local ice-cream parlour and indulged ourselves. I had what they called a large "Jim Dandy" which Tom flatly insisted I couldn't possibly manage to eat, but I did, and thoroughly enjoyed it. Pig that I was!!Elsie told me that her and Bob had a week's holiday and had booked a coach trip to Vermont and asked if we would like to go with them if it could be arranged. I of course jumped at the chance, so off we went. It was apparently really an organised holiday for Senior Citizens but happily we were all allowed to join in.

The scenery on the journey was beautiful and we were accommodated in a wonderful Swiss type chalet hotel called "The Matterhorn" which was used mainly for skiers in the winter. It also boasted a very large swimming pool in the grounds for the summer visitors. All the rooms were large and extremely comfortable each with its own en-suite.

Downstairs there was a delightful dining room, and a bar where everyone helped themselves to drinks on an 'honour' payment basis. The food was delicious served by a happy friendly staff. I really loved the breakfast times when I indulged in pancakes smothered with Maple Syrup. There were a number of planned excursions for everyone and we thoroughly enjoyed them. I remember there was a musical evening at a small theatre where some of the patrons were called upon to sing and entertain, and where Bob had to go up on the stage, dress as a lady and sing, and during which he really had everyone doubled up with laughter at his antics.On the final day at the hotel there was an outdoor Barbeque type party by the swimming pool and Bob was in the pool swimming, and also diving off the top diving board. Tom, who couldn't swim a stroke, just had to prove himself by joining in and going up and diving too. Luckily Bob was nearby when he landed in the water to help him, and get him safely out of the pool.Bob, who had had heart bypass surgery a number of years previously, never gave up on any physical type of enjoyment or exercise, insisting that he would not be treated like an invalid. We returned to Elsie and Bob's house by coach the following morning everyone having been given a framed group photograph of their time spent at "The Matterhorn".

The month's holiday in America with Elsie and Bob soon flashed by and we travelled back to England by plane, leaving at night. This time, determined not to know hardly anything at all about the journey, I craftily took two sleeping pills and happily they worked. I only really came to my full senses when the plane had safely landed at Heathrow. I am still convinced that the best and only way to travel is by ship, and that aeroplanes should never have been invented.

Chapter 20

I had been suffering a number of aches and pains in my limbs and joints for some time and in the early eighties I was diagnosed with Poly-Arthritis, which got worse as time went by. My walking ability was badly affected and limited, and I had to use a walking-stick everywhere, even inside the flat. It wasn't long before I found that almost every activity was extremely painful and difficult, sometimes impossible. I was informed and persuaded to apply for a Mobility Allowance which after a while I did. A Ministry doctor visited and examined me and I was then classed as disabled and received the allowance, also a disabled badge for Tom's car giving him free road tax and parking for driving me around. The local council department for helping disabled persons then visited my flat and installed hand-rails and necessities, including an extra banister for the outside stairs which at the time helped a lot. At the local hospital I received a long course of Hydrotherapy sessions in the warm exercise pool, and many instructions and information regarding suitable daily exercises to perform and so forth. I visited a shop selling products for the disabled and purchased a number of things including an electrically powered armchair to enable me to sit down and get up more easily. I'm afraid that Tom, although of course he wasn't paying for them, gave me the usual hassle saying that none of these items were really necessary. They were, and I'm glad I bought them. In fact when he visited my flat afterwards he always sat himself down in the armchair and never wanted to move, but still would not buy himself a decent armchair for his own comfort in his house. Surprisingly, both to myself and his family, I did manage finally to persuade him to do away with his old fireside chairs and purchase two three seater settees to accommodate his company when necessary, although we started out to buy a three piece suite which he as usual refused. So his family and callers no longer had to find themselves dining chairs (if there were enough available) to sit on. (I had an awful lot of trouble trying to persuade Tom to buy new net curtains too. This he stolidly refused to do relying on his next door neighbour to supply him with her old ones, which she was kind enough to continue to do.)Another purchase I made, strongly against Tom's better judgement, namely an electric shower which I had especially fitted and happily used, was after a couple of months taken up by him. Asking me for full details of where I had obtained the shower, Tom later had one fitted and installed in his house, even though he had been so strongly against the very idea of having one at all in the beginning, insisting that such a thing was completely unnecessary. That was Tom!(And yet at times with friends, family, and acquaintances, he would go exactly the opposite way happily buying everyone quite expensive gifts. It was amazing, and utterly confusing.)

Bella lived near Burnham-on-Crouch a yachting place I loved and Tom and I visited her several times and spent the day there. One summer she let us have one of her chalets at St. Osyth's near Clacton for a week's holiday and I thoroughly enjoyed myself. It isn't a beautiful sea-side place, but has it's fair share of charm and fresh air. I'm afraid that Tom, used to the lovely Devon sands and countryside I suppose, also the attractions of European excursions, was not very impressed with .St. Osyth"s at all, except for it's Sunday morning markets.

He therefore was glad to get home and never offered to return. Sometime later when Bella's husband Jim died Tom took me to his funeral, and several years afterwards, sadly, to Bella's, where I met up with the rest of my family except of course Elsie and Bob. They weren't forgotten however, as I gave a lovely floral tribute in their name. Tom took photographs of Bella's funeral and we sent them to Elsie.

Although Tom had received a large redundancy sum upon his retirement, he did not want to spend it and still bitterly complained about bills including house rent and so forth. He also worried continually that the council, because his house had three bedrooms, might decide to evict him and place him into a small flat, so that they could use his house for another family. Listening to all these worries and complaints so frequently, I had a brainwave and stupidly, when the 'right to buy' materialized, suggested that I should buy his house from the council with the money I had saved during my working life hoping to buy mother and myself a small bungalow, plus some of my mobility allowance. Tom happily agreed to this with the condition that he should continue to live there for the remainder of his life. He even went so far as to offer to pay me a weekly rent, which I of course refused. Because he had lived in the house for forty years there was a good rebate, so the money I had saved was adequate. Tom took me to the bank and I drew out all my savings and bought the house in his name as agreed. I admit that I was hoping that after a time we would be able to sell the house and buy a two bed roomed bungalow together somewhere in the country or by the sea. Unfortunately, when Tom told his daughter that I had bought the house she was very annoyed and said that if she had known, her and her husband would have taken out a second mortgage and bought the house themselves, thus providing both of them with a "golden handshake" later on. She hated the idea that I now owned the house and asked me somewhat indignantly if they would still be allowed to visit and stay there as before. I agreed that it would be fine and that they should carry on as usual, knowing that she was just trying to make me feel bad. She was unwilling to let the matter rest however, and was the instigator of a lot of ill feeling throughout the family, and arguments between Tom and I during the years that followed.

Chapter 21

Tom had a gall bladder operation in a local hospital and after spending a week there requested a period of convalescence afterwards which was granted. I helped him to get ready for the hospital car which was to take him, and asked him if he was sure that he had put his money-belt on around his waist. He pulled up his pullover to check and we were both shocked to discover that his shirt was covered in blood. His operation scar had opened up. I grabbed the telephone and rang the hospital but they weren't at all concerned or interested as he had been discharged they said. So I then rang his doctor and explained what had happened and she sent an ambulance right away. He was taken to one hospital but they had no bed, so he ended up at another some distance away. By this time the wound had become infected and Tom had to spend several weeks being treated in the hospital. I travelled by Dial-a-ride to visit him frequently, in fact Bella's daughter Eileen who was visiting me from Brighton for a day, drove me there once in her car. When he eventually left hospital he went to stay with his daughter in Devon for a couple of weeks. There were a number of occasions, when Tom felt ill and asked me to call the doctor, one was when a Locum was on duty and visited him. After seeing Tom the doctor came down the stairs and said that there was nothing actually wrong with him. Then looked at me and said "You look far worse than him".

I asked him then if Tom could have a Home Help to do the housework and he agreed and dealt with it. Then Tom rang me early one morning saying that he didn't feel well. When I went to see what was wrong he was obviously quite poorly so I rang his doctor and an ambulance was sent at once. Tom was having a heart attack and was kept in hospital for some weeks. I notified his family who were abroad on holiday at the time, and went to see him by taxi every day until he was discharged. Then I collected him by taxi and brought him home. He had suffered two minor heart problems at previous times. There were a number of occasions when Tom had day hospital visits for Bronchoscopies and when he was brought home had to go to bed because he felt so ill. Once he complained that he was in pain all over after one of these so I telephoned the hospital doctor who had given him the Bronchoscopy and told him. He was very nice and laughingly said that you always felt as if you had been in a "Rugby scrum" afterwards, and not to worry. All in all poor Tom had quite a few health problems until he ended up with Prostrate Cancer, which was of course a terrible worry. He received daily Radiotherapy and was finally told that he was clear of the disease, but the cancer kept returning. He also had a hearing problem and I accompanied him to one hospital to be tested and receive a hearing aid which after trying to use once or twice he discarded, complaining that it distorted every sound. He then continued to have all the media items i.e., television and hi-fi units roaring loudly throughout the house.

I received word one day that my half-brother Alec, whom I hadn't seen or heard from for some time since hearing that he and his wife had opened up a café, was in hospital after having a minor heart attack. I sent him a get-well card and best wishes and when he recovered and was back home, he telephoned me. From then on we were in constant touch with each other. I was very pleased about this especially as he, his wife, and family visited Tom and I on a number of occasions. (When Tom would, as usual, 'hold Court' as I called it, by standing in the middle of the room with his back to the fireplace, and talk continuously not letting anyone else get a word in. Which both embarrassed and annoyed me, but amused Alec immensely.) Alec now lived in a lovely area of Surrey and his daughter, now married, and his oldest son who was also married, lived nearby. His youngest son had long since emigrated with his wife and family to Australia where he was said to be doing well. Tom and I received an invitation to Alec and Elsie's (same name as my sister) Golden Wedding Anniversary, and ten years later to their Diamond. During those ten years however, I spent some very happy times at Alec and Elsie's house in Surrey, very happy. Alec would come down with Elsie in his car and they would drive me back with them for a week or two before bringing me home again. While I was with them I spent some time with his daughter and also with his son. They all made me so welcome it was as if I'd never been away from them at all, and that I still belonged with my own family. It was a wonderful feeling, 'like coming home again.'During my visit with Alec his son Norman, who showed me his computer, advised me to either buy a Lap-top or Word Processor for my writing, rather than the typewriter I was using. He said it would be a lot easier. So, after thinking about it, I sent for a Word Processor and began using that. I found it quite complicated but did use it from then on.

For most of my adult life I had, and still do, suffer quite a lot with indigestion. Way back Dr. Dean sent me for a Barium Meal test thinking that it might be an ulcer, but the result came back negative. He then regularly prescribed the usual medication and I was fairly careful about my diet. Over the years I had quite a few Barium tests, even the horrible Enema a number of times, but nothing was diagnosed. I was quite worried then when I found it more difficult to eat much solid food at all, and lost my appetite feeling also nauseas most of the time. Even when I went shopping with Tom, especially at the butchers, I found that I had to stay outside the shop as I couldn't even stand the smell, let alone the sight of the meat, yet the shop was kept so spotlessly clean and the floor always covered in fresh sawdust. During a fairly short space of time I lost five stone in weight and became extremely weak and quite haggard in the face. I had an Indian doctor who just sat at his desk holding a pen poised above a prescription pad, and as I entered his surgery each time would simply ask "Well, what do you want?" and begin writing, almost before I had time to answer. Never once was I examined or given a blood test all the time I was in his practice. After a number of visits about my weight loss and eating problem which he happily ignored, I faced up to him and said that things couldn't go on like it and that I wanted a hospital appointment. He appeared quite surprised but gave me a letter for the hospital. Tom had been nagging at me for ages to change my doctor as that one was useless, as amongst many previous visits to him regarding an extremely painful breast abscess, where he did nothing at all until his wife who was present, and was a nurse, forced him to send me to hospital to drain the abscess.Apparently all Tom's family, and my friends and neighbours were convinced that I was suffering from cancer, because of my appearance and weight loss. I attended the local hospital many times to see a doctor who was considered to be especially good and was given innumerable tests including endoscopies, CT. scans, blood tests etc. which of course took several months, (I was even tested for Addison's disease). The doctor was assisted by an excellent woman doctor, so kind and caring, who told me quite frankly that her partner was convinced that I had a tumour, and was determined to find the answer. I was given some tablets when they also found that I had inflammation of the stomach and they helped quite a bit. One morning I received a letter from the hospital saying that the CT. scan had shown up a black mass in the Pancreatic area and that I must attend for an extra special Endoscopy. I did, it was a most unpleasant experience but luckily I was told that nothing unusual was shown. The hospital visits continued in this way for some months until it was decided that my gall bladder was badly infected and had to be removed and I was seen by a surgeon. During all this time I had become good friends with the woman doctor Elizabeth who was very religious, and the wife of a vicar, and who had helped me a lot both emotionally and mentally. The surgeon I saw decided to remove my gall bladder by Key-hole surgery because of my arthritic problems, but I had to sign a consent form for both types of operation., in case the Key-hole type proved unmanageable. However, it was successful and afterwards I stayed at Tom's for a while until I recovered. It was his turn to look after me, and he did. Alec rang me everyday to find out how I was and to cheer me up, it was lovely to hear from him. Upon a subsequent check up visit with the surgeon he informed me that there was a problem with my digestive system, he said it could even be a Hernia as my stomach kept sending the acid back up into my gullet. He said that he wouldn't investigate further at the moment though in view of all the anaesthetic already used for the operation, but that I should eat little and often and have a very bland diet. (Twelve years later after yet another Barium meal, it was finally discovered that I was suffering from a Hiatus Hernia). I gradually began to find it a little easier to eat and put the weight I'd lost back on again. I discovered that the Hiatus Hernia also affected your voice making it quite croaky. Sometime later I saw sense and changed my doctor and registered with Tom's, which I discovered was the best thing I did as Dr. Kalkat was and is a brilliant and caring doctor.

One evening my new friend Dr. Elizabeth took me along to what she said was a 'Healing Service' in a church she knew and it was most interesting. She lived in London at that time but then her husband was given a new Ministry in Canterbury and although I no longer saw her we kept in touch by correspondence. Elizabeth sent me a small book that her mother had given her entitled "God Calling", it contained daily Christian thoughts, also a little wooden palm cross which had come from the "Holy Land". We still exchange greeting cards and remain good friends. I started to attend the small local church and made a number of friends there. The vicar lent me quite a few video recordings of the Biblical stories, most of which I have now purchased myself on DVD's. I went to a commenerative service held at a church in Romford one Sunday evening with one of the women from my church in memory of my mother and her husband. I was then confirmed by the Bishop of London at St. Patrick's church in Barking on the 11th of December 1983. When I had difficulty getting to the church because of my walking problem, the vicar gave me Communion in the flat every Sunday. I became friends with a woman of my own age at the church called Peggy who was previously a teacher and lived with her mother She became a special friend and visited me at the flat often, particularly on a Sunday morning after the service, frequently bringing me small bouquets of flowers or ferns from the garden. She also encouraged me a lot in my writing. Peggy was a wonderful person, a really true Christian. She helped everyone she could in many ways. Peggy was only happy helping , going around doing things especially for the elderly, tending their gardens, anything. She was like a sister to me and I grew to love her and looked forward to her visits. She was an active member of the church in many different ways , even firmly keeping the children attending Sunday school in order, and going around the district collecting for Christian Aid and so forth. She was very kind and caring in everything she undertook. Peggy's interest was Geology and she was of course very intelligent. She belonged to a Geologist's club and when she had to give a speech she brought the draft to the flat and read it out to me first for my opinion. Not that I had any idea at all on the subject matter, I'm not that clever, but she just wanted to know if it all sounded alright. It was extremely interesting. The time came however that she became ill and was absent from church and from my flat for some time. I wrote to her and received a reply saying that she did feel terribly ill but the doctor's did not seem to know what was wrong. Then one day I was told by the vicar that she was in hospital undergoing exploratory surgery. That was on her birthday and I asked Tom to take me to see her, taking a birthday present with me. We entered the given ward and asked a nurse where her bed was. The nurse looked a little startled, then showed us into a small room and disappeared. The Sister then appeared bearing cups of tea which she handed to us.. I was amazed at the kind reception but was both shocked and upset when she explained that although Peggy had awoken safely from the operation she had died shortly afterwards. I was heartbroken and couldn't stop crying. The Sister stopped in the room with Tom and I for a while until I recovered enough to leave. Apparently they'd found that Peggy had terminal Cancer and of course would have suffered a great deal before her life ended, so in one way her death could be called a blessing, but to those who loved her so much it was most cruel. A short time after the funeral the vicar arranged a special memorial service for Peggy at the church which everyone attended, even Tom. It was all terribly sad. Later I wrote a short verse of my own in memory. I still miss her very much.

Chapter 22

During all this time because I'd bought Tom's house, his eldest daughter frequently rang him to advise him that everyone thought that because he'd paid rent to the council for forty years and thus obtained a good rebate on the purchase price, he was entitled to a part share in the house. The telephone calls kept coming over the weeks and months and finally they caused a big row between Tom and I. I had had enough I said and that our association had finished. I walked out of the house and returned to my flat determined to have nothing further to do with Tom. As I left I asked him to bring me up my share of the groceries I'd paid for as I would of course need them. A short time afterwards he came up to the flat and broke down completely in tears saying that he really wanted us to stay together and pleaded with me to make up with him again. It upset me to see him in tears and so unhappy and I spent some time comforting him and agreed to remain close friends. Because I am a 'soft touch' and was so sick and tired of all the hassle, not to mention sorry that I had been stupid enough to buy the wretched house in the first place, I promised him half of the property. (At the time of buying the house it had nothing at all to do with his family, simply an agreement between the two of us.) (Later when Tom decided that a new roof was needed and doors etc., I paid half towards the cost.) Apparently, when he told his daughter sometime later she was very surprised and quite delighted as she hadn't dreamt that he'd get as much as half and had only expected a small portion. After that they couldn't wait until Tom had made it all legal in his will and testament and given each of them a copy of the will. Upon reflection Tom could quite easily have bought the house himself with his redundancy money instead of giving it all to his two daughters, which he did!!!

When I told my half-brother Alec the story he advised me to get my name on the deeds as a joint owner of the house lest I lose the lot, so I did this as soon as I could by getting Tom to write to the solicitor handling the house purchase.

Edith and Peter still lived in the council house that mother had obtained for them years ago. Their three daughters had all married and the youngest one lived in America. Two of the daughters bought the council house that their parents were living in and allowed them to continue living there. When Peter died a number of years later Edith remained in the house alone. I never saw her at all even though I was told that she visited my church quite often in a Council Limousine, why I don't know, and I lived only five minutes away. I know that she did not care for Tom but there was no reason that she couldn't call in my flat for a brief visit. Not that I really minded as we weren't all that close and had nothing in common except for being sisters. I eventually saw her on Alec's 80th birthday. His daughter Pearl had telephoned me a couple of weeks previously and asked me to arrange a dinner party at a restaurant near where I lived for all his family, myself and Tom as a birthday surprise. I did this and she also invited Edith. The dinner was a great success , and everyone really enjoyed themselves, Alec was delighted. A very happy, still active 80 year old. I remember that as I went to the door of my flat to say goodbye to them all Edith asked me if I would like to live in Sheltered Accommodation as it would be better for me. Not having heard of this type of accommodation before,

I immediately became suspicious as she was the one who had put me into a Home earlier, and said "Definitely not". She did not pursue the subject.

I had one or two telephone calls from Edith after that and a number of years later heard that she was suffering from Alzheimer's disease. Later on I was told that her daughter had put her into a Home as she couldn't be left living alone any longer.

My nephew John, George's son, and his daughter Sophie visited me several times. They met Tom of course and happily consumed many of his (prize) cakes. It was lovely to see them. Sophie was tackling our 'family tree' at the time and worked hard on it eventually producing quite an excellent document on most of our Ancestors. They still visit me at the flat when they can and Sophie who travels the world quite a lot, always remembers to send me a postcard from wherever she is. My niece Eileen, Bella's daughter, also visits me from Brighton whenever she can.

I was in frequent contact with my sister Elsie in America by correspondence and telephone and she told me that Bob was having memory problems and was also beginning to suffer from Alzheimer's disease which was of course most upsetting. He got worse after a few years and sadly Elsie had to have him admitted to a nursing home. She told me that she often visited him in the Home but he never even recognised her and it of course broke her heart. They had been married for fifty seven years or more. Bob was 79 when he died in the nursing home of pneumonia. It was very sad as I too had loved Bob very much and recalled the fun we had all shared together years ago. Elsie now lived alone. She did have her children living near her, all now married with families of their own. Later, her youngest son, now divorced, went to live with her so she was no longer lonely.

Chapter 23

Tom's youngest daughter came over from Ireland and stayed with him for six months taking a job in London. She and her husband were now divorced, they had no children, and she wasn't to sure about staying in Ireland any longer. She did however, return and came back to see Tom fairly frequently for long weekends. Tom's youngest son who was only in his forties died suddenly from a heart attack and Tom was of course very upset, as were the rest of the family. His eldest daughter now had her widowed mother-in-law living with her who had the beginnings of Alzheimer's disease. She and her husband took frequent trips abroad on holiday so she asked Tom to have her mother-in-law at his house with him when they were on holiday. He of course agreed, although by now he himself was having quite a few health problems due to age, and was also experiencing memory lapses etc., and needed quite a lot of help, so the request was rather unfair. However, his daughter and husband would bring the mother-in-law down to Tom's house and then happily disappear on holiday somewhere. I helped to care for the elderly lady while she was at Tom's but at times it was quite a problem and hard work. Eventually, when it became quite noticeable and obvious to the whole family, they stopped expecting Tom to look after her and found her a place in a Home.

I had many more invitations to visit Alec and Elsie over the years but Alec, because he was nearly ninety years old now could not drive all the way and through the London traffic to collect me as before, and as I wasn't confident enough to travel by train or coach by myself I never went to see them, which I really regret. I rang him frequently however, and later on discovered that he was ill and that Pearl, his daughter was looking after him. Every time I spoke to Alec on the telephone he told me that he felt terrible. I sent 'get well' cards and flowers to cheer him, but he never appeared to get any better, and one day his son Norman rang me to say that he didn't think that Alec would last much longer and if I wanted to see him I should go as soon as possible. I desperately wanted to go and asked Tom if he would drive me there but he didn't think he could manage the distance. He mentioned the problem to his eldest daughter and husband over the telephone and they agreed to take both of us as long as I paid for the petrol used. I was quite willing to do so and gave them £100 to cover all their expenses. It was a long journey and when we arrived Pearl met us at the door and took Tom and I in to see Alec who was sitting, in his pyjamas next to his wife Elsie. I was really shocked to see the difference in them both, due of course to age, but poor Alec really looked dreadfully ill. He didn't know Tom at all, but recognised me immediately and seemed so pleased that I'd come to visit him. I hugged and kissed him, telling him how much I loved him, and also that mother loved him dearly and he was so pleased. (he'd confessed to me a couple of times in the past that he thought mother never cared for him, to which I'd told him that it was nonsense to think such a thing.) I had great difficulty holding back my tears so he wouldn't see them as we talked. I couldn't stay talking to him very long as he was very tired, so kissed him again and he told me that he really loved me very much before I left him and walked into the other room in tears. Norman was there to hold me close and comfort me and then I disappeared into the bathroom to cry my eyes out until I recovered enough to come out and join the others. I never saw Alec again before we left to go home as he was resting. Pearl and Norman promised to let me know how he was by telephone, and we had to leave. It wasn't very long before I got the call to say that dear Alec had passed away, and I was heartbroken. I sent two floral tributes, one from Elsie and family, and one from me. Tom's daughter and son-in-law drove us to the funeral where we met the rest of the family and some of Alec's friends. It was a very sad, tearful occasion. I remember that in the funeral car I heard Alec's wife Elsie say, "I knew he was ill, but never thought he would die." She was, and looked, lost They had been married for seventy years. She lived with Pearl afterwards who took great care of her even when she became most forgetful. I believe Elsie was a year, or two older than Alec and I wasn't surprised, but quite sad, when Pearl telephoned to tell me that she too had now passed away. A grand old couple, sadly missed. To think that as a child I was ever afraid of Alec and nervous of Elsie, is now beyond belief!!

Chapter 24

Quite suddenly Tom's eldest son reappeared on the scene after over twenty years or more absence and introduced the whole family to Spiritualism which they all took to, 'like ducks to water'. They all completely believed everything they were told by the Medium, even Tom. He desperately wanted me to join in, telling me that my mother probably had a message for me, but I wanted absolutely nothing to do with it. Talking to the 'dead' is quite wrong, and definitely against religious beliefs. His son and wife now lived in a bungalow in the Cambridge area, where the so-called Medium held her meetings. Being the eldest member of the family he also decided that he should now run everything concerned with it, including Tom, who raised no objection. I tried to get on with him, but just could not stand him at all, he was so big headed and obnoxious to my way of thinking, obnoxious in every way. I often wondered where he was when Tom was so ill etc., and could have done with help of some kind, but no, it seems he turned up when he thought that Tom was now old and something would be in it for him if he was around. A wicked thought for me to have I know, but. ,... can you blame me?From then on Tom spent one or two weeks with him and his wife at their home in Cambridge now and again, sometimes joined by the rest of the family, all of course visiting the Medium whilst there and sometimes taping her words for all to hear and share.

Tom's eldest daughter and husband took him to Normandy one year to see the war graves of his friends and all around the places he had been when fighting during War World 11, and he thoroughly enjoyed it, although many of the memories were of course very sad. Being an old soldier Tom was always talking about the things that had happened to him on D-Day and thereon, and all his mates. I'd heard most of his stories over and over, and over again. On his return home from the visit he brought me back an ornamental glass bowl of hand-made silk roses which is extremely pretty and still stands on my coffee table.

Tom was getting more and more forgetful as the days went by and I had to remind him of practically everything. He also became quite difficult at times. Cantankerous is the word I think, also very argumentative. Life at times became quite impossible. Yet, on other occasions he could be fairly reasonable and helpful. Used as I was to being with elderly people I still found it a bit of a trial. We got by however, and remained close friends. (That is, when his family didn't interfere).

Chapter 25

My next health problem was unfortunately a Prolapsed Bowel, which was very serious and required a Major operation. I was so ill I couldn't go down to Tom's house as usual in the afternoons or anywhere else apart from the hospital and doctor surgery visits. Dr. Kalkat was extremely helpful in every way, as was poor Tom who did everything he could. I was practically bedridden. I couldn't even sit down anywhere, and even had to stand at the table to eat my dinners etc., The pain and discomfort was terrible. I just had to wait however, until there was a bed available in our local hospital for the operation. This turned out to be a very long wait of practically eighteen months, including two last minute cancellations. I did even try to go private but discovered that the operation would be carried out by the same surgeon who advised me to wait for the National Health to deal with it. Tom's youngest daughter helped all she could by frequently ringing the hospital admissions department and even the surgeon's secretary to try to hasten the operation. I just had to 'hang on' and wait, which I did. However, whilst I was trying to wait and cope with this health problem I was continually besieged with telephone calls from Tom's eldest daughter advising me how to get help from the Social by asking for a Carer. I'm sure she meant well, but the frequent phone calls telling me what to do began to drive me crazy, especially as I was feeling so ill. I'm afraid that finally I lost my temper and told her that I wasn't stupid and was quite capable of running my own life. The calls then stopped. I was grateful to her however, for previously introducing me to a company which provided customer's with frozen meals on a regular basis, as my Arthritic hands were no longer capable of preparing and cooking food. I still rely on this company for my meals. Tom continued to come to the flat for lunch every day and brought me in a sandwich and tea and sat by the bedside with me to eat his as well, there wasn't much else he could do except do his best to listen to my problems and issue words of comfort. He did have a row with the surgeon's coloured second in command about the long delay for my operation, which was not forgotten by the victim for a long, long time, who when I eventually went into the hospital never failed to ask me where the "Colonel" was on each and every bed visit!

I did ask the Social for help after a while when I was still waiting for my admission into hospital, and after answering thousands of never ending questions during one of their frequent visits, I was given a Carer who called twice a day, seven days a week. She was a black African, very intimidating to say the least, with a rather frightening appearance. Her spoken English was also quite poor. I wasn't at all keen, especially when she immediately changed the arranged calling times to suit herself. I was asked by the Social Worker why they were changed and she wasn't too pleased with my answer and apparently had strong words with the aforesaid Carer, who, when I opened the front door to her the following morning was looking so angry and fierce, I expected her to produce a Spear and attack me with it! I was spared though, no Spear, and was brusquely told that she would not be coming to me anymore as she had been given another area in which to work. I was so relieved. My next Carer was also a black African, it seems that white British Carers (as well as white British nurses) are extremely sparse nowadays, the country having been inundated with immigrants. This one however was entirely different in every way, could speak quite good English and had been in this country for some time, and was good at her job. We seem to get on well together, she is still with me now, her name is Annet. When she gets any time off, I am always supplied with another Carer, they are all usually black Africans except for Carnel who is a West Indian, has been in this country since she was two years old, and is just like one of us in every way except of course, colour.

It happened eventually, after two previous cancellations, I finally received a telephone call late one afternoon to say that there was a bed available in the hospital for me as long as I got there well before 7 pm. Expecting an ambulance to collect me I waited, and waited, none came. Tom was also panicking and made a few urgent phone calls to the hospital who at last said that there wasn't an ambulance available. He was not going to let me miss this opportunity however, good old Tom, and wrapped a blanket around me, took one of the pillows and somehow or other I managed to lie on the backseat of his small car. We got to the hospital just before seven only to find that they weren't at all ready for us and we had to stand and wait in the ward for a number of hours. It was midnight before the bed was made ready and I was permitted to lie in it. A flustered coloured nurse quickly informed me that my operation was taking place the next day and gave me some opening medication to take for my bowels, which unfortunately never worked. In the morning I discovered that, as seems to be the case nowadays in England, it was a mixed ward much to my distaste, not only in sex but also in race. There were all Nationalities in patients as well as nurses, doctors and hospital workers in general. (There is no need to travel at all nowadays, everyone in the world can be found here, especially in this area.).My operation I was told would take place at about 2 pm. I lay there and waited. I must admit I was terrified. I'm not at all brave about operations and dislike hospitals immensely. I just wanted the whole thing over. I knew it had to be done I just couldn't go on the way I was. I expected to die under the anaesthetic, but had quite accepted the fact. I think that Tom's family all expected it too, that's the impression they gave. I had had a number of minor operations in the past but had been told that this was a big one. During the morning I was visited by the Surgeon accompanied by about six or more students to whom he had great delight showing my problem saying, "I don't expect you've seen anything like this before." That made me feel a lot better! Later some of the students returned asking for my permission to watch the operation,- as if I cared, anyway I wouldn't know who was there would I? (hopefully). The Surgeon was the same one who had previously removed my gall bladder. I was also visited by the Anaesthetist who asked a number of questions.Just before 2 pm. I was wheeled into the Operating Theatre and anaesthetised.The next thing I knew was that I was being awakened by the Anaesthetist and a nurse and in terrible pain. I remember crying out over and over with the pain, almost screaming, and the Anaesthetist repeatedly injecting me with Morphine until he said that he'd given me enough to suit a young man, and could give me no more. The Surgeon came over saying "Is there a problem?". They were talking about putting me into a special care ward if the trouble persisted but luckily the Morphine finally began to take effect and the pain got a little better, so I was returned to the same surgical ward I was in before.Later I was informed that they had managed to replace the bowel but had been unable to repair the muscles, so that there was the possibility of yet another Prolapse if I became constipated. Very comforting I'm sure. Dr.Kalkat therefore provides me with the necessary medication to prevent this happening. Two or three days later I was given a chest Xray and a nurse then put tight long white socks on my legs which I was told not to remove. I discovered later that both these things should have been done before the operation.... I also had an injection put into my stomach every night to prevent blood clots.

All in all I spent a month in the hospital during which time I discovered many things. They were badly under staffed and had nurses and carers/volunteer workers of very many nationalities most of whom could hardly speak or understand English. They had no time at all for the elderly patients., and no love, simply wished them elsewhere. The hospital food was practically uneatable and by the time it reached you mainly cold. The patient buzzers were hardly ever answered, if at all. There was very little privacy for both sexes. The ward appeared to be very noisy at night with new patients being wheeled in and loudly attended to by doctors and nurses, many coming from A & E. The regular night nurses made a lot of unnecessary noise as well. There was very little sleep, if any. There was also the risk of catching other health problems, diarrhoea was one and quite prevalent in the ward at the time and we all contracted it. A young woman in a bed nearby got a nasty infection after her operation and was still there when I was discharged. Every patient it seemed had a mobile telephone which they used continually, ignoring any comments made by the nurses, which of course added to the chaos. Visiting time was I may say the worst time of all for shattering any kind of peace. Most of the patients had at least five or six visitors around their beds at one time and it was bedlam! You will probably think that I was jealous not having any visitors at all after the first day or two before Tom's family took him on holiday, but you'd be quiet wrong. I do happen to enjoy peace and quiet. Something you just cannot get in hospital!Mind you, the patients all appeared to feel sorry for me being the only one who never had any visitors, and often sent one or two of their own visitors across to my bed with some of the edible gifts they'd brought, which was very nice of them and which I never refused.I got on well with all the patients and very soon with all their visitors who did all they could to befriend, and help me if necessary. I feel I should mention that when Tom did pay me one or two visits directly after my operation, he only spent a few minutes with me before walking around all the other beds in the ward befriending all the patients, laughing and joking with them all, quite forgetting that he'd come to see me. On one of these visits, feeling quite neglected and rather annoyed, I shouted across to him to remind him that I was still there, causing a great furore of laughter and agreement in the ward. But, that was typical I'm afraid of Tom who loved new faces and letting everyone know he was about.All the time I was in the hospital I had to wear the Catheter which was fitted during the operation and it was most uncomfortable. I was told by a nurse that the bowel and bladder are close together and an operation on one could upset the other. I was visited by the surgeon several times and also by his coloured assistant who never forgot to enquire about the "Colonel" and his whereabouts.My continual request to be allowed to go home was ignored for sometime. The surgeon stating that I needed long term care, and his assistant asking me who would care for me if I went home. Even the nurses when they came to me to give out pills etc., would look at me and say, "Ah, you're the one who just wants to go home." My plea was that well known throughout the hospital. The Occupational Therapists took such an interest in me that when I did get home they called on me the very next day to check the flat to see if there were any improvements they could make to help, and then provided me with more up to date disability equipment. It wasn't very easy to obtain a discharge and get out of the hospital though as it was decided to send me on to another hospital and I was visited by a doctor who told me that he had a bed available in a local hospital where I could be cared for. I told him no. I was going home. About a week later I had another visitor from this hospital whom I also very firmly refused. They gave up in the end and I came back home to my lovely little flat, where I found loads of mail, and also loads of peace at last! The Social had been informed of my return so Annet turned up at her usual times to take care of me. I also rang my doctor's surgery to tell them, and the receptionist said "Welcome home", which really made me feel as if someone had missed me after all. Dr. Kalkat also seemed to be pleased to see me and was glad that I hadn't gone on to another hospital and had returned home instead. Said that he'd had quite a lot of letters from the hospital about me. I hope they gave me a good 'report'. Amongst all the unopened mail I found at home were a large number of lovely 'Get Well' cards from the family, most of which were from my sister Elsie.

Chapter 26

When Tom returned from his holiday he came to the flat to see me and find out how I was. Things then got back to normal with him coming up for his lunch every day. I no longer went to his house in the afternoons for dinner in the evening but just continued with the frozen meals which were delivered fortnightly to my flat. I was not yet strong enough to venture out apart from the problem with the stairs, of which there were fourteen to climb to the flat, and at Tom's house stairs to conquer to the bathroom and toilet, all of which caused me considerable difficulty due to my Arthritis. Tom also came to the flat of an evening and later I made both of us some Ovaltine. He often dozed off after drinking his and I had to awaken him to send him home before it got too late. Annet was still coming to me twice a day and so far is continuing to do so. She always carried out some grocery shopping for me once a week and now and then I asked her to get one or two things for Tom, as it seemed that he was rather neglecting himself where his evening meal was concerned. He told me that he was eating jam sandwiches instead of cooking himself an evening meal. I did try to persuade him to have the frozen meals like me thinking that they would do him more good, but he wouldn't listen. I was quite worried about him but he could be very stubborn.

Tom's family visited him fairly often now and one day he told me that they had decided to do his house up so that the value of it would increase considerably. They removed the bath and installed a Walk-in Shower, and put new kitchen cupboards in etc., Tom paid of course. They did work hard and later on when I could just about manage it he took me there to see the improvements. It looked very nice.

Several months later when I felt a lot stronger I decided to buy a Lap-top and asked Tom if he would take me to the local" PC. World" showroom. Once there, after Tom had rooted out the Manager and engaged him in about an hour's unnecessary argument, I purchased my "Toshiba" Lap-top, now called "Tosh" by me, plus printer and all the necessary equipment. I had never even been close to a computer before or printer, and hadn't got a clue how to use them. Even the keyboard is slightly different to a typewriter. I had to wait a few days for the technician to arrive and install it and then work out how to use it.... Annet was very interested and encouraging and gave me a text book from "Learn Direct" covering the beginner's introduction to a computer. I had also bought an instruction book with the Lap-top which I had some difficulty understanding. I was however, very eager to learn everything and use the machines as soon as possible, and am now extremely glad that I did. "Tosh" is a very good friend to me. In time I got Broadband from BT, they just sent me all the cables and plugs to fit myself, which I may say was the very limit. I had no idea what to do and could not get anyone to sort it out. Eventually I told a solicitor friend my problem and she came along to the flat and fixed it all up for me. I now go 'on line', get lots of information, even from the NHS Direct about any health problems that occur, and check that my GP. is treating me the correct way and telling me everything, much to Dr.Kalkat's amusement. He tells me that I have an 'enquiring mind' which I confess is quite true. I shop on line, send e-mails, and even copy the CD's lent to me by the Mobile Library, apart from carrying on with my writing. Yes, I'm so glad that I took the plunge and invested in my Lap-top. Of course with my Arthritic problem I cannot sit at it too long, I have to get up fairly often and move around, the same as I do with my Typewriter or Word Processor, or of course I would get a lot more writing done than I seem to, I'm sure.

It was only about a month or more later that Tom became ill. I went down to take care of him and sent for Dr. Kalkat who came right away and prescribed some medication. I continued to care for him administering all the pills given . I was there one day when his youngest daughter rang him as she did fairly often and I answered the call and told her that he was ill. She said that she would take the next flight over from Ireland, which she did arriving the following day.

She then took over the caring and I continued to visit every day to help and see how he was. His condition appeared to vary from day to day. Sometimes he was like his old self, other's he was delirious which reminded me of how he was all that time ago when I nursed him through Pneumonia. Dr. Kalkat did everything he could for him but he had to go into hospital as he was so ill. Tom's eldest daughter and husband came and stayed at his house also when told about his illness. They all went to visit him in hospital every day. I wanted to go too but although I could get a taxi to the hospital I needed someone to help me to the ward as it was some distance from the entrance. I did ask his eldest daughter for this help but she said that she just couldn't manage it. So, as I had always done when he was in hospital I rang the ward daily to find out how he was. The sister and staff were very nice and answered my queries. A couple of times they even allowed him to come on the phone and talk to me and then he sounded fairly well and was very pleased to hear me. However, when the eldest son was told of Tom's illness he came and joined the rest of the family and upon visiting Tom in hospital told the staff not to accept any calls from me. He then had the audacity to ring me at home and forbid, actually forbid me to ring the hospital for news anymore! He was such a nice man!! I did not take orders from him however, so continued to ring for information. The hospital did take them it seemed and refused to answer my enquiries. Tom's youngest daughter was the only member of the family who appeared to think I should know everything and she rang me each time she visited him to tell me how he was and what exactly was happening.I think he was in the hospital for about three weeks. They gave him another Broncospy and also removed some fluid from his lungs I was told, but instead of rallying he appeared to just give up and died. He was eighty five years old, but it still came as a terrible shock. Tom had always been so strong and active and had survived a number of serious illnesses on previous occasions. It was very hard to believe and accept, but I had to.

I had lost a very dear old friend and companion and I shed many tears. It took a long time to come to terms with it. Tom and I had been together for well over thirty years not of course without differences of opinions and minor upsets, but nevertheless as close friends.

When my friends and family heard about Tom's death they all sent sympathy cards and flowers. Elsie, my sister in America immediately wrote and told me that I needn't stay here on my own she would love to have me live there with her, which of course I would have been very happy to do but my health problems prevented this. It would have been impossible to pay America's health prices. I recall that even Annet sent me a large basket of beautiful flowers to try to cheer me up. My home-help came by taxi with me to Tom's funeral where we saw all his family and one or two of his neighbours. It was a very sad occasion and strangely enough was held on the 11th of November, Armistice Day, very fitting I think for an old veteran but none the less still very sad.

I did not visit Tom's house again. One or two family members came to the flat once or twice to bring me a few of my photographs etc., and a couple of framed pictures of a younger Tom when he was in uniform. The contents of the house were shared out amongst his family I believe and his son-in-law visited me to ask if I wanted to leave my flat and go to live in Tom's house as it was suggested in his will. The place could not be sold if I did until I too passed away. I thought about it quite quickly and decided against the idea altogether. I was happy to stay where I was at the time, and it would not benefit me to move there. As I refused the offer they were quite able to go ahead with the sale of the property so they put it into the hands of Estate Agents, and then returned to their own homes.

I continued to live in my flat (my Sanctuary, or so I called it), and gradually came to terms with Tom's death in the way we all have to. I must admit that I did miss him quite a lot but as time went by it became easier. Dr. Kalkat was most caring and visited me to see how I was getting on. He suggested that I joined the local luncheon club and perhaps one of the other clubs for the elderly to help me pass the time and relieve any loneliness I might be experiencing. I declined the offers and told him that I was happier on my own spending my time writing, listening to music, reading or at the last, watching TV. I said that for me, and it is still quite true, there just aren't enough hours in the day to do everything I want to do and that I never feel lonely at all. He is not only my G.P. but I class him as a good friend now, which he continues to be. I do manage to go out occasionally as I have a 'Taxi Card', belong to Dial-a-ride, and have bought myself a disabled electric Scooter which I call "Pegasus" and which I have grown quite fond of, if that's at all possible.

About the Author

Leslie Adams was born in E.London. She came from a very poor working class family. She has written verse, articles and short stories. This is her first non-fiction book. She still lives in E. London.